The BIG FLORIDA

REPRODUCIBLE

Activity Book!

BY CAROLE MARSH

This activity book has material which correlates with the Next Generation Sunshine State Standards.

At every opportunity, we have tried to relate information to the History and Social Science, English, Science, Math, Civics, Economics, and Computer Technology NGSSS directives.

For additional information, go to our website: **www.gallopade.com**

Published by
GALLOPADE™ INTERNATIONAL
800-536-2GET
www.gallopade.com

TECH CONNECTS

Connect to a world of related information, activities, and more at:
www.gallopade.com/techconnects.html
password: activity

Gallopade is proud to be a member or supporter of these educational organizations and associations:

ASCD ABA AMERICAN BOOKSELLERS ASSOCIATION APPL NCSS

A Word From The Author

Florida is a very special state. Almost everything about Florida is interesting and fun! It has a remarkable history that helped create the great nation of America. Florida enjoys an amazing geography of incredible beauty and fascination. The state's people are unique and have accomplished many great things.

This Activity Book is chock-full of activities to entice you to learn more about Florida. While completing puzzles, coloring activities, word codes, and other fun-to-do activities, you'll learn about the state's history, geography, people, places, animals, legends, and more.

Whether you're sitting in a classroom, stuck inside on a rainy day, or–better yet–sitting in the back seat of a car touring the wonderful state of Florida, my hope is that you have as much fun using this Activity Book as I did writing it.

Enjoy your Florida Experience–it's the trip of a lifetime!!

Carole Marsh

The Florida Experience Series

My First Pocket Guide to Florida!

The Big Florida Reproducible Activity Book

The Fabulous Florida Coloring Book!

My First Book About Florida!

Florida Jeopardy: Answers & Questions About Our State

Florida "Jography!": A Fun Run Through Our State

The Florida Experience Sticker Pack

The Florida Experience! Poster/Map

Discover Florida CD-ROM

Florida "GEO" Bingo Game

Florida "HISTO" Bingo Game

Florida "BIO" Bingo Game

Florida Regions

Let's visit the natural regions of Florida.

Fill in the blank crossword with the names of the five regions.

Coastal Lowlands
* Industrial
* Resorts

Western Highlands
* Sparsely settled

Tallahassee Hills
* Rolling Hills

Swamp Lands
* Okefenokee
* Everglades
* The Big Cypress

Central Highlands
* Thousands of Lakes

Fabulous Flag!

The Florida state flag has a white background with diagonal red bars. In the center of the flag is the Great Seal of the State.

COLOR FLORIDA'S STATE FLAG

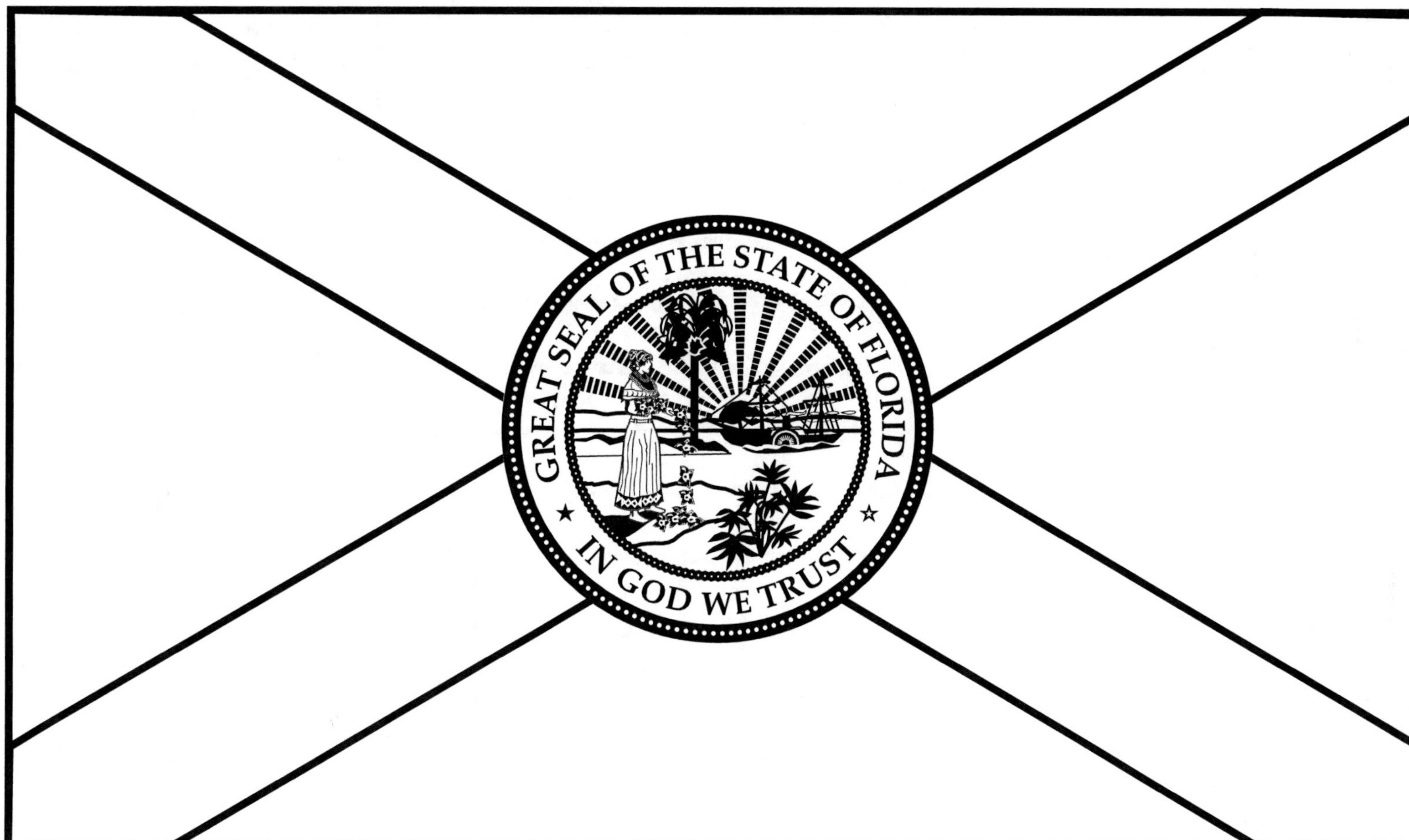

Florida's state motto is "In God We Trust."

In the Beginning...
Came a Settlement

King Philip II of Spain sent an able seaman named Menendez to drive the French out of Florida. He arrived in 1565, attacked the fort, and founded St. Augustine, which became the first permanent settlement in what is now the United States.

Help the ship find its way from Spain to St. Augustine.

MARINE LIFE Word Search

Florida is well known for the variety of marine life that inhabits its waters.

See if you can find the names of some of the marine life that swim in and around Florida's waters.

TARPON	MANATEE
SAILFISH	LOGGERHEAD
SPINY-LOBSTER	SPANISH MACKEREL
SHRIMP	SEA TROUT
CONCH	SHARK

```
E L O P I S K N M S P S H A R K
P S M A N A T E E G O E T Q E S
S F K L O G G E R H E A D I P E
A S P I N Y L O B S T E R L T A
I H G R M K C N S S H R I M P T
L S Q T A R P O N L R C C A W R
F N W G O A C E S Q K O D N O O
I A E S H R A M P D G N U A I U
S F M P K N N L C T F C H T W T
H K R Q M D C G B I J H E E T N
S P A N I S H M A C K E R E L T
```

Buzzing Around Florida!

Find the answers to the questions in the maze. Write them on the lines. Follow a path through the maze in the same order as your answers to get the bee to the beehive.

Florida is bordered by ____________ bodies of water.

The shape of Florida is a ____________________ .

Florida is in ____________ America.

American ____________ were the first people to live in Florida.

The ____________ Ocean borders Florida on the east.

The ____________ _____ ____________ are to the south.

Florida has many __________________ off its coast.

The ____________ _____ ____________ borders Florida on the West.

When you look at the geography of Florida it has no __________________ .

Florida is the state that is farther to the ____________ than any other state.

Florida has almost 8,000 ____________ .

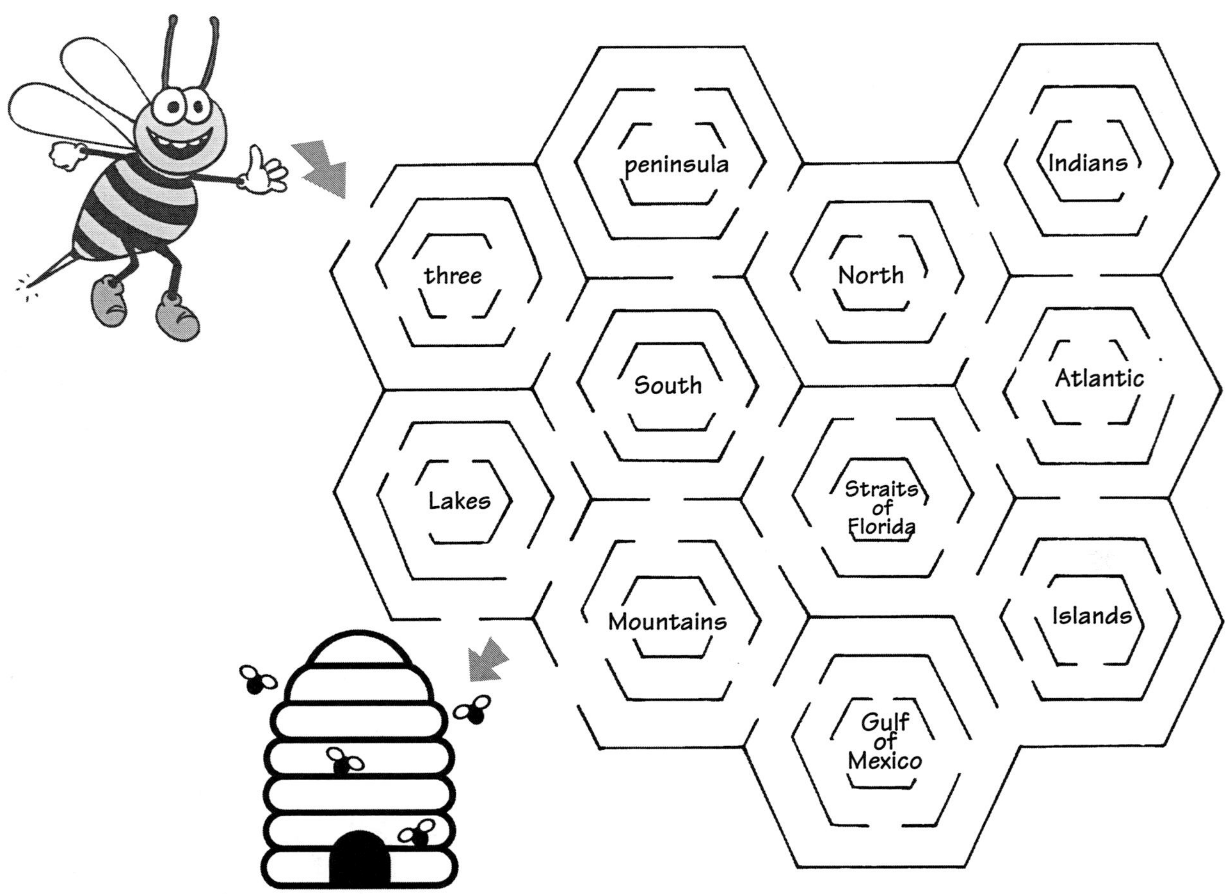

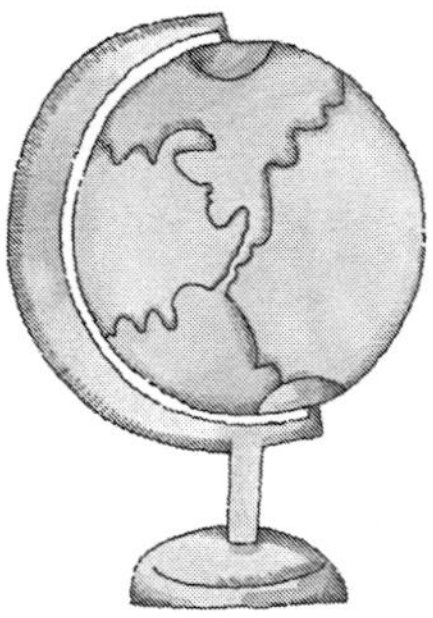

Florida Hispanic Immigration

Since Fidel Castro's communist takeover of Cuba in 1959, more than 800,000 Cuban immigrants have come to Florida. Much of this immigration has given Florida a Hispanic flavor, especially in southern cities like Miami. Recently, Cuban immigrants have been joined by immigrants from other Hispanic countries like El Salvador, Colombia, and Venezuela. This has helped to make Florida a mecca of Hispanic banking, trading, and culture. Just in Miami alone, approximately 60 percent of the residents speak a language other than English at home.

How much do you remember of what you just read?
Try filling in the blanks below to complete the sentences.

1. Fidel Castro took over ______________ in 1959.
2. Since Castro came to power, more than ______________, ______________ Cuban immigrants have come to Florida.
3. This has given Florida a ______________________ flavor.
4. One Hispanic country that has sent immigrants to Florida is ____________________
5. This has helped make Florida a mecca of Hispanic ______________, ______________________, and ____________________ .
6. Just in Miami, ______________ percent of the population speaks a language besides English.

Answers: 1. Cuba, 2. 800,000, 3. Hispanic, 4. El Salvador, Columbia, or Venezuela, 5. banking, trading, culture, 6. 60

Rhymin' Riddles

I am a state in the South, a peninsula you see;
A lot of my historic sites tourists come to see.

What am I? ______________________________

I lived on the land in Florida before the Spanish did roam;
Saplings covered with tree bark near a river were my tribe's home.

What am I? ______________________________

I'm a city in Florida, land of sun and palm tree;
I go by the name of Tallahassee.

What am I? ______________________________

I'm an important part of this country's race;
Shuttles from here lift off into space.

What am I? ______________________________

On the Georgia-Florida border I sprawl;
Within my backwaters snakes do crawl
Lake Okeechobee is here, Florida's largest in size;
But alligators call me a "paradise."
What am I? ______________________________

ANSWERS: Florida, Indians, capital, Kennedy Space Center, Okefenokee Swamp

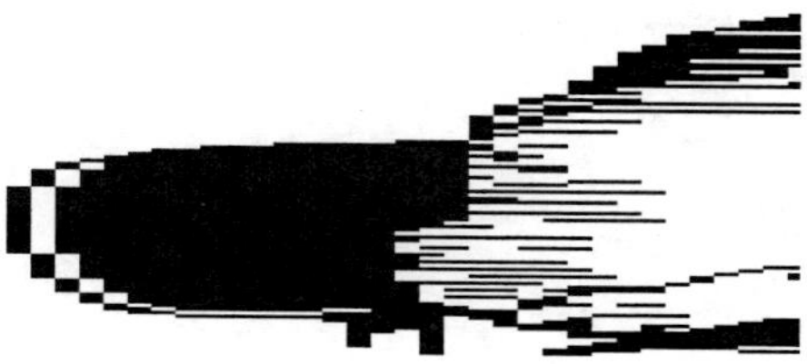

Florida Wheel of Fortune

See if you can figure out the Wheel of Fortune-style puzzles below! "Vanna" has given you consonants in each word to help you out.

1. **A state north of Florida**
2. **Ocean east of Florida**
3. **____________ of Florida**
4. **Body of water west of Florida (__________ of Mexico)**
5. **A state northwest of Florida**

☐	☐	☐	R	☐	☐	☐	
☐	T	☐	☐	☐	☐	☐	C
S	☐	R	☐	☐	☐	S	
☐	☐	L	☐				
☐	L	☐	☐	☐	M	☐	

ANSWERS: 1. Georgia 2. Atlantic 3. Straits 4. Gulf, 5. Alabama

Famous Floridian Females

The state of Florida is blessed with some fabulously famous females! For example, Mary Mcleod Bethune taught at mission schools in Florida from 1895 to 1904. Bethune was also the founder and first president of the National Council of Negro Women. Bethune's contributions to African-American women, as well as Americans in general, is unparalleled. Another famous African-American woman was Zora Neale Hurston, an American anthropologist and writer who in the 1930s worked with the Harlem Renaissance, an African-American arts movement. Hurston was born in Eatonville and became America's most important collector of African-American folklore. Trailblazer, Jacqueline Cochran, was an aviatrix who held more speed, distance, and altitude records than any other modern flier. Born in Pensacola, Cochran was voted the world's foremost female flier in 1937, 1938, and 1939 by the International League of Aviators. Cochran also organized and led the Women's Airforce Service Pilots (WASP) in World War II. Marjorie Kinnan Rawlings lived on a farm in Cross Creek, located in central Florida. Her novel, *The Yearling,* won her the coveted Pulitzer Prize in 1939 and was later made into a movie. Did you know that tennis great, Chris Evert-Lloyd, was born in Fort Lauderdale? Ranked the world's number one tennis player six times, she was inducted into the Tennis Hall of Fame in 1995. Wow! What an awesome sampling of just a few of Florida's famous females!

Now see if you can fill in the blanks to name something significant about these famous females. Follow the example:

Jacqueline Cochran	Female pilot who set many records
Chris Evert-Lloyd	______________________________
Mary McLeod Bethune	______________________________
Marjorie Kinnan Rawlings	______________________________
Zora Neale Hurston	______________________________

Sing Like a Florida Bird Word Jumble

Arrange the jumbled letters in the proper order for the names of birds found in Florida.

BALD EAGLE
CRANE
PELICAN
HERON
EGRET
PARROT
FLAMINGO
MOCKINGBIRD
STORK
WOODPECKER

E D L A B L A G E __________

A C N I E L P __________

R O R T A P __________

O K S T R __________

T E R G E __________

D O C K B M N I R G I __________

G L A I F N M O __________

E O H N R __________

D O O W P C E E K R __________

E A N R C __________

ANSWERS: bald eagle, pelican, parrot, stork, egret, mockingbird, flamingo, heron, woodpecker, crane

Let's Get Regional!

Florida is divided into six natural regions. The Coastal Lowlands include the entire coast and the Florida Keys. The Western Highlands in the Panhandle are relatively hilly. In the north-central part of the Panhandle you find the Marianna Lowlands. Rolling hills and thousands of lakes make up the Tallahassee Hills. Two separate swamplands make up the fifth and sixth region, the Central Highlands and the Swamplands.

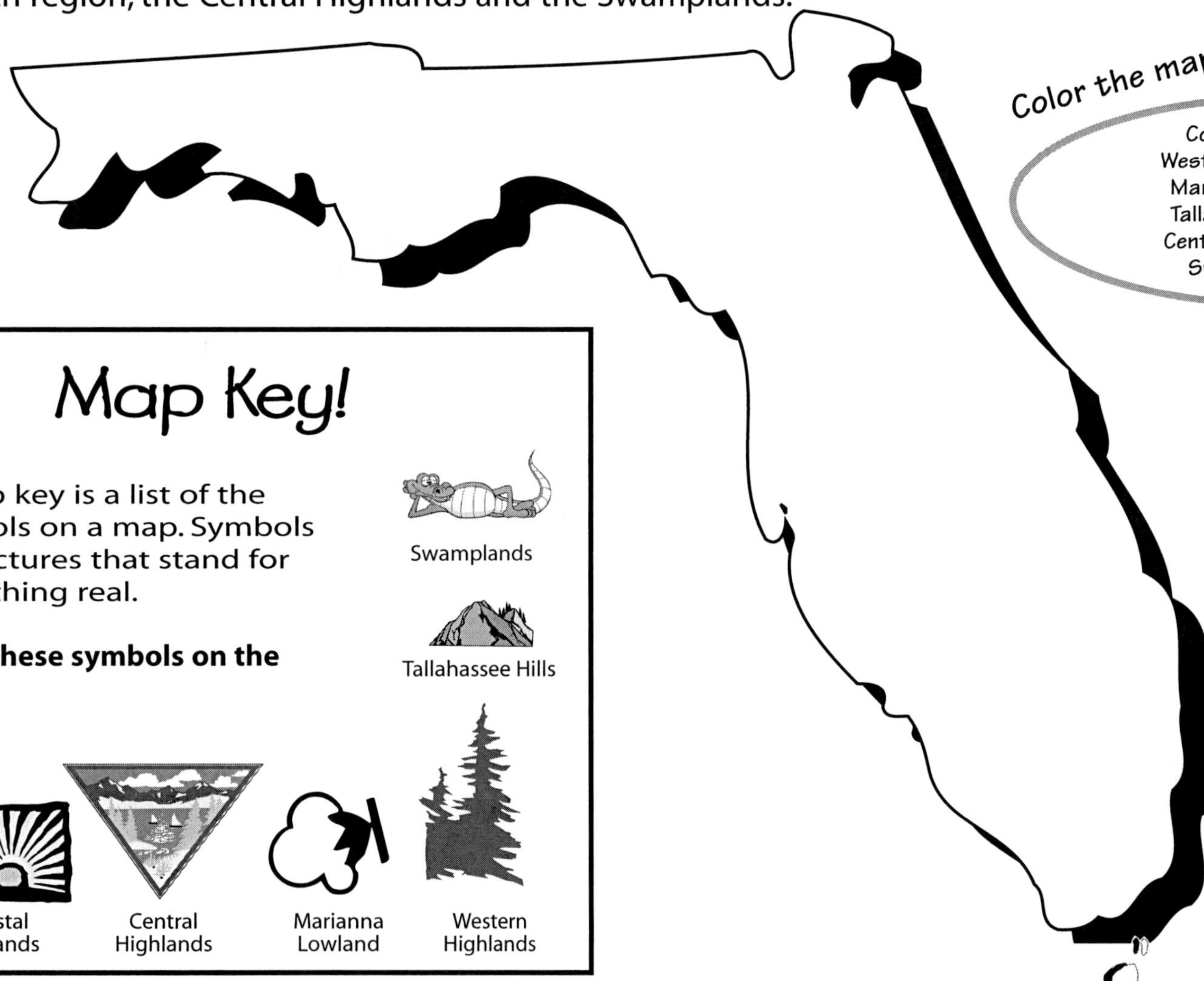

Color the map as follows:

Coastal Lowlands - blue
Western Highlands - green
Marianna Lowlands - red
Tallahassee Hills - yellow
Central Highlands - brown
Swamplands - purple

Map Key!

A map key is a list of the symbols on a map. Symbols are pictures that stand for something real.

Draw these symbols on the map.

Swamplands

Tallahassee Hills

Coastal Lowlands

Central Highlands

Marianna Lowland

Western Highlands

Florida Turtles

Florida's beaches are nesting sites for many sea turtles of the world. From spring until fall, female turtles come on shore after nightfall to lay their eggs. They dig holes above the high tide line on the beach, then lay anywhere from 40 to 180 eggs in the holes, which are covered with sand for protection. Over several weeks, the eggs are warmed by the sand and the sun until the baby turtles break out of their shells, dig their way to the surface, and make a mad dash for the sea. Many are eaten on the way to the water by birds, raccoons, crabs and other predators. Once in the water the turtles still are not safe. Diving birds and fish love to make a meal of the baby turtles.

COLOR KEY

R = red **B = blue**
Y = yellow **G = green**

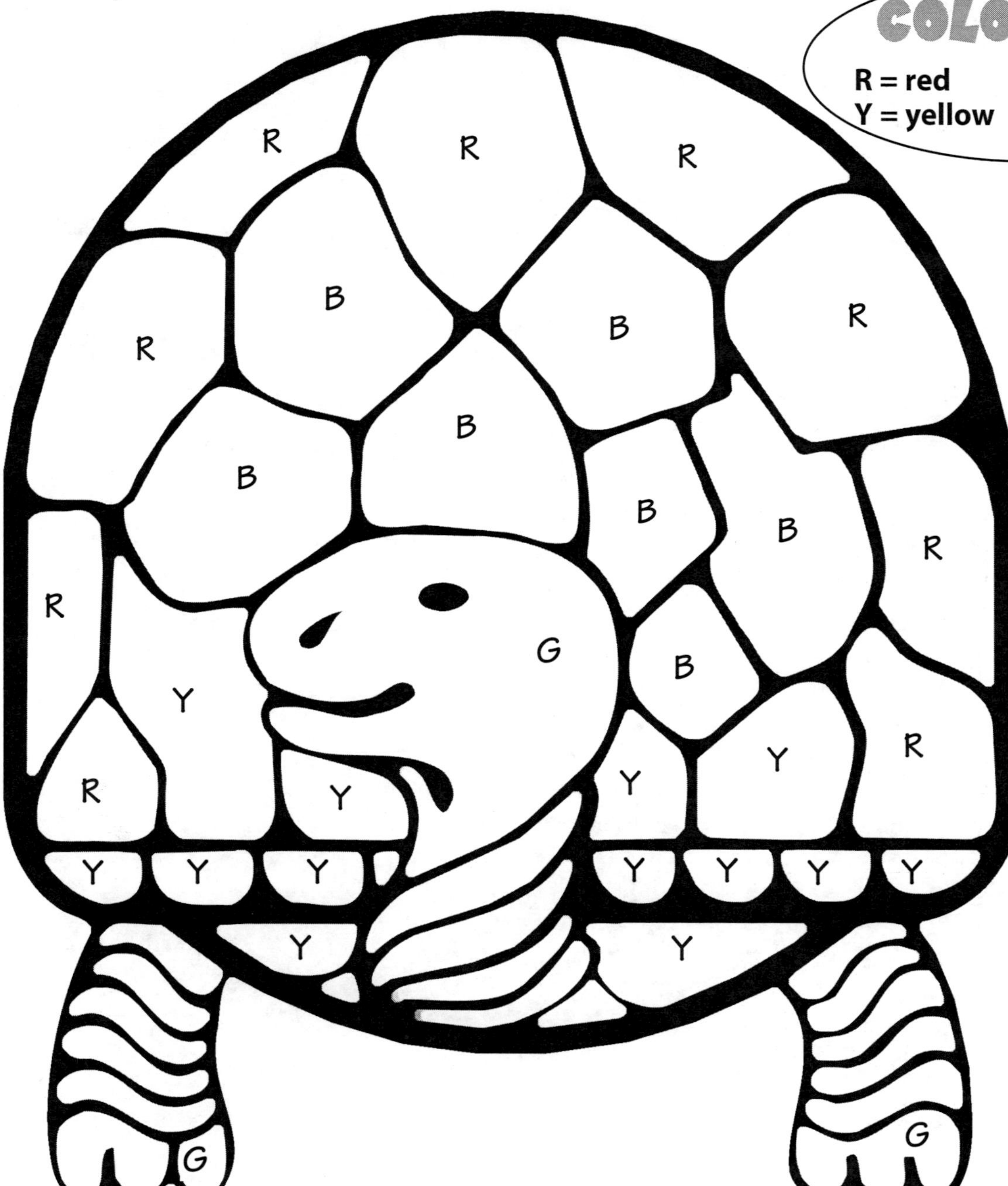

How many spots are on this turtle? ______________

ANSWER: 29

American Alligator Dot-To-Dot

Once, the American alligators were nearly extinct because people hunted them for their hides and meat. Adult alligators have very strong jaws, 80 teeth, and a brain which is only the size of a walnut! Unlike us, an alligator's eyes, ears, and nostrils are on the top of the head. This enables them to see, hear, and smell when swimming just below the surface of the water with just the top of their heads exposed.

Alligators are usually not aggressive towards humans, but can be if they are surprised or if the human comes too close to an alligator's nest. Always be careful not to swim in the murky waters or after dark in areas where alligators are known to live.

Connect the dots below to see an American alligator.

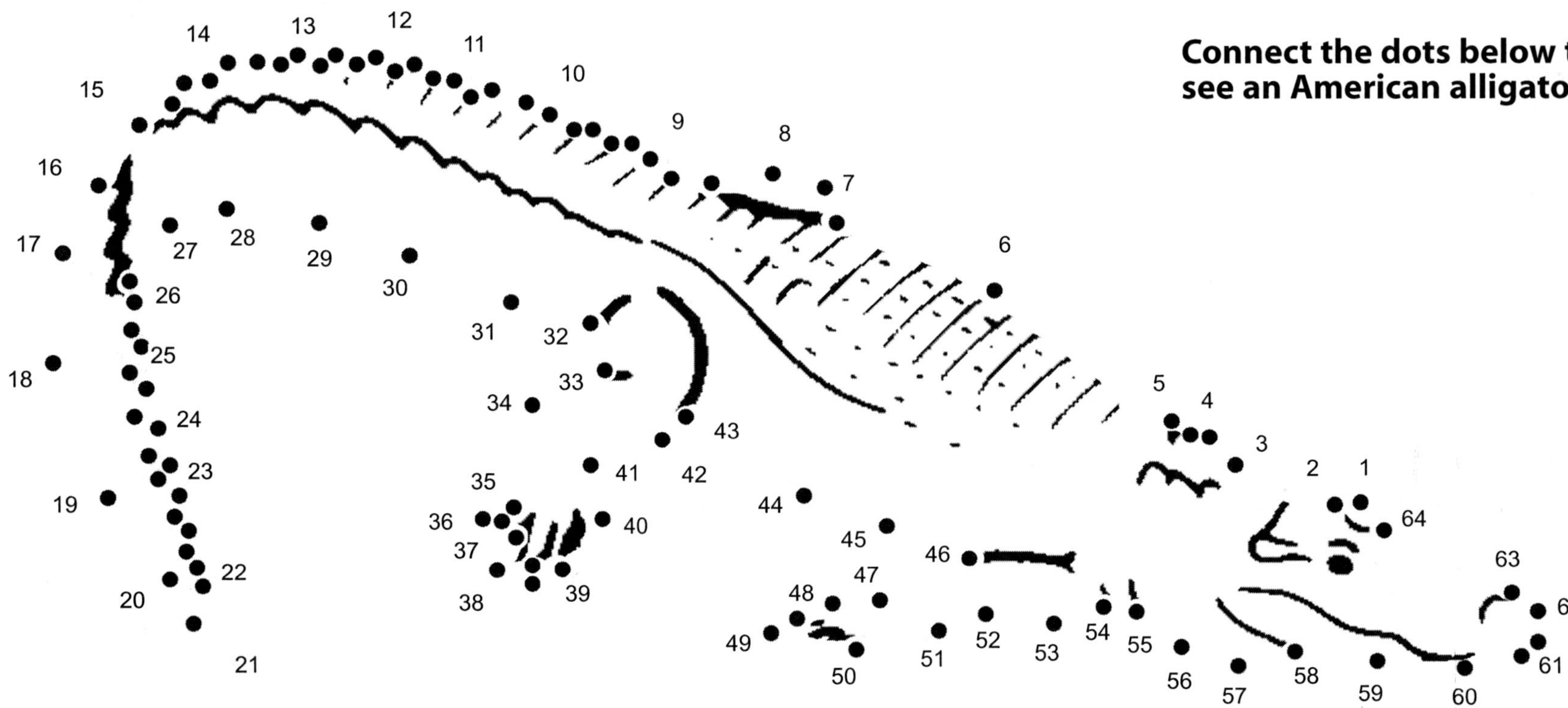

Eat Your Florida Produce

Find the names of fruits grown in Florida in the word search below.

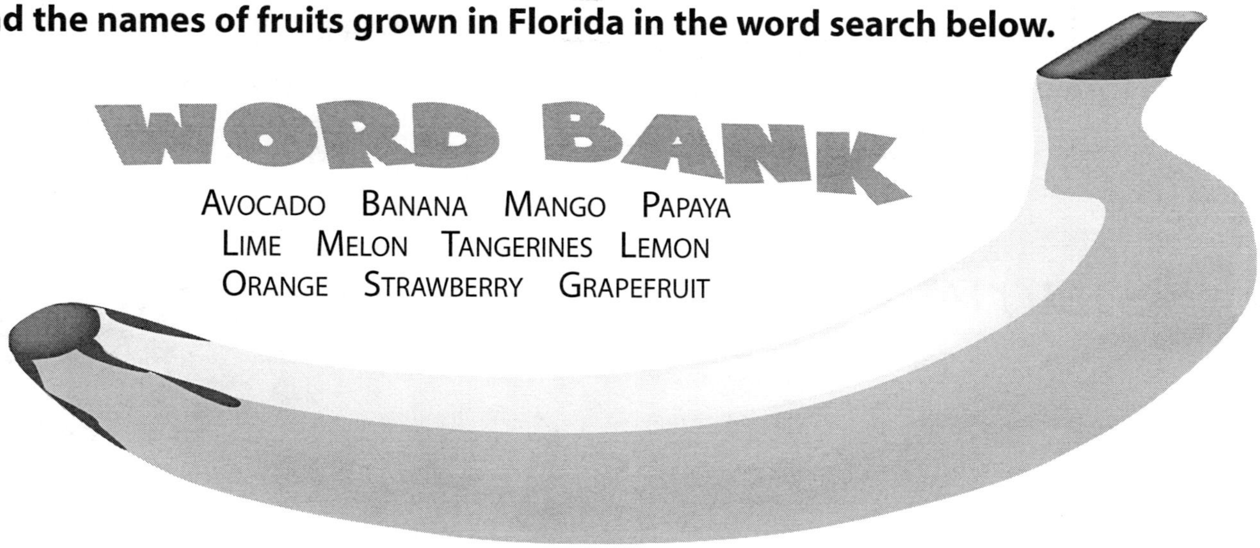

WORD BANK

AVOCADO BANANA MANGO PAPAYA
LIME MELON TANGERINES LEMON
ORANGE STRAWBERRY GRAPEFRUIT

```
A B S D P G M E L O N X R T D
V B A N A N A S I E R E H T E
O R A S P Y N O U C A N S S E
C U M A A I G L L T I W N T E
A B E T Y H O A N A Y E L R L
D Y E L A L E M O N S H S A A
O D L I M E S A G G B C D W R
S C G F X D R A B E J E E B N
A G A S Y O U C O R A N G E S
R N I H T L A E R I E H T R R
E Y O U R E A D Y N F O R R B
E C D R T L C E F E J I K Y C
B C D L Z X E F G S R B A C J
G R A P E F R U I T P O N L K
```

Florida, The Sunshine State!

Match the name of each Florida state symbol on the left with its picture on the right.

Nickname

State Bird

State Animal

State Insect

State Flower

State Tree

State Saltwater Fish

State Shell

State Drink

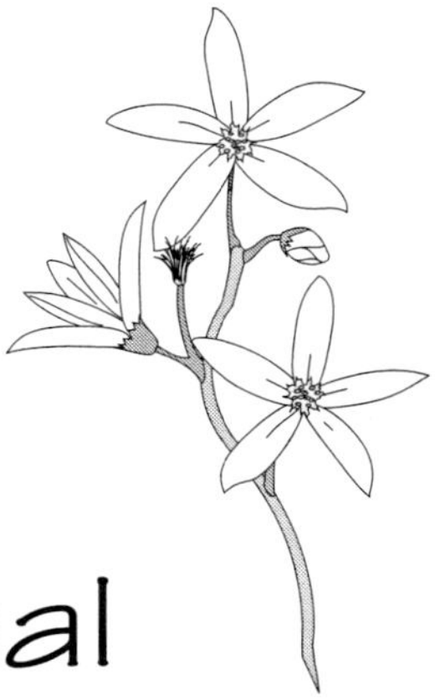

Ollie's Orange Grove

Spanish explorers brought oranges to Florida. In 1579, Pedro de Avilés saw wild orange trees growing all over the St. Augustine area. Farmers began to grow oranges in the early 1800s as a commercial crop. Most oranges are now grown in south-central Florida, just west of Orlando. Oranges are Florida's most important crop. Florida is the largest producer of oranges and orange juice in the world, next to Brazil.

How many oranges do you see in Ollies' grove? ☐

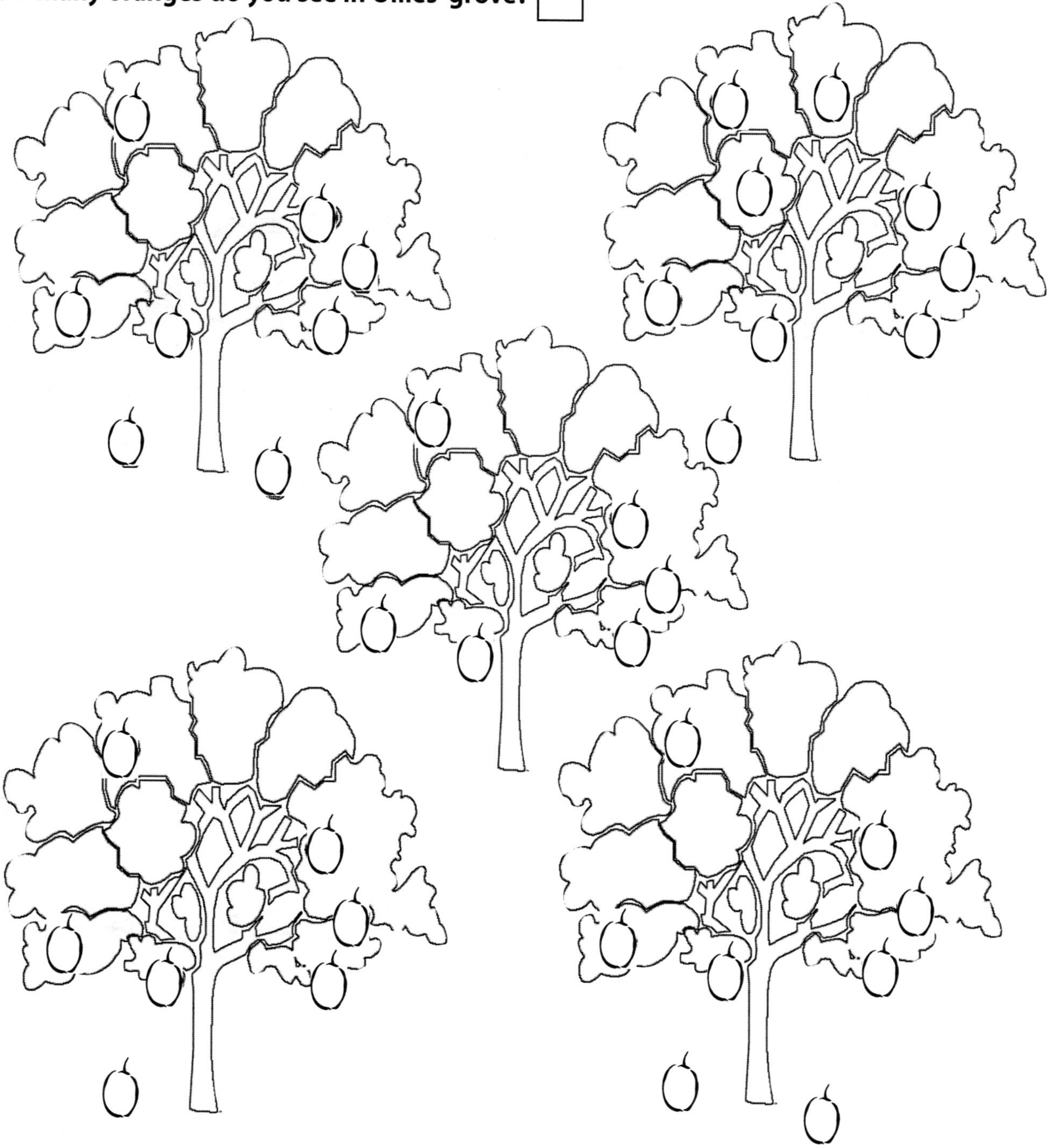

If all the oranges grown in Florida each year were laid end to end to end, they would go 2 million miles into space! That's like taking a round trip to the moon 4 times!

ANSWERS: 38 Oranges

A Drive In Daytona

You can walk on the beach. You can ride bikes on the beach, but did you know you can drive on the beach in Daytona? If you drive at less than 10 mph, you are allowed to take your car on the hard beach sand. Earlier in the century, 13 auto speed records were set on Daytona sand. Today, the Daytona International Speedway (well-removed from the beach) hosts major professional auto races. NASCAR auto racing is the most popular sport in America today.

Put race car numbers on these race cars and color them.

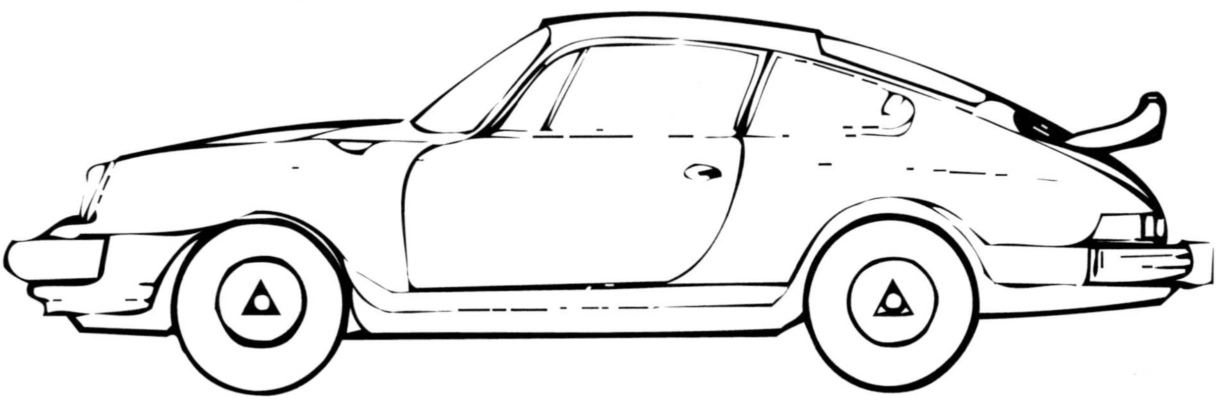

FLORIDA SPELLING BEE

Good spelling is a good habit. Study the words on the left side of the page. Fold the page in half and "take a spelling test" on the right side. Have a buddy read the words aloud to you. When done, unfold the page and check your spelling. Keep your score. Good luck spelling all these Florida FUNdamental words!

Flagler	**1.**	____________________
Fort King	**2.**	____________________
Florida Keys	**3.**	____________________
Fort Lauderdale	**4.**	____________________
fishing	**5.**	____________________
frozen orange juice	**6.**	____________________
Flamingo	**7.**	____________________
fishtail fern	**8.**	____________________
fiji fan palm	**9.**	____________________
Fontaneada	**10.**	____________________
Fakahatchee	**11.**	____________________
foureye butterflyfish	**12.**	____________________
fox squirrel	**13.**	____________________
fuzzy-wuzzy airplant	**14.**	____________________
fire sponge	**15.**	____________________

"Little" Mermaid

Manatees are gentle, slow-moving sea mammals. Homesick sailors would often mistake them for mermaids because their flippers looked like little hands! Manatees are endangered animals, and there are only about 1,000 of them left in Florida waters. Almost half of all manatee deaths are caused by humans and boat propeller blades.

Help the manatee find the warm safe waters.

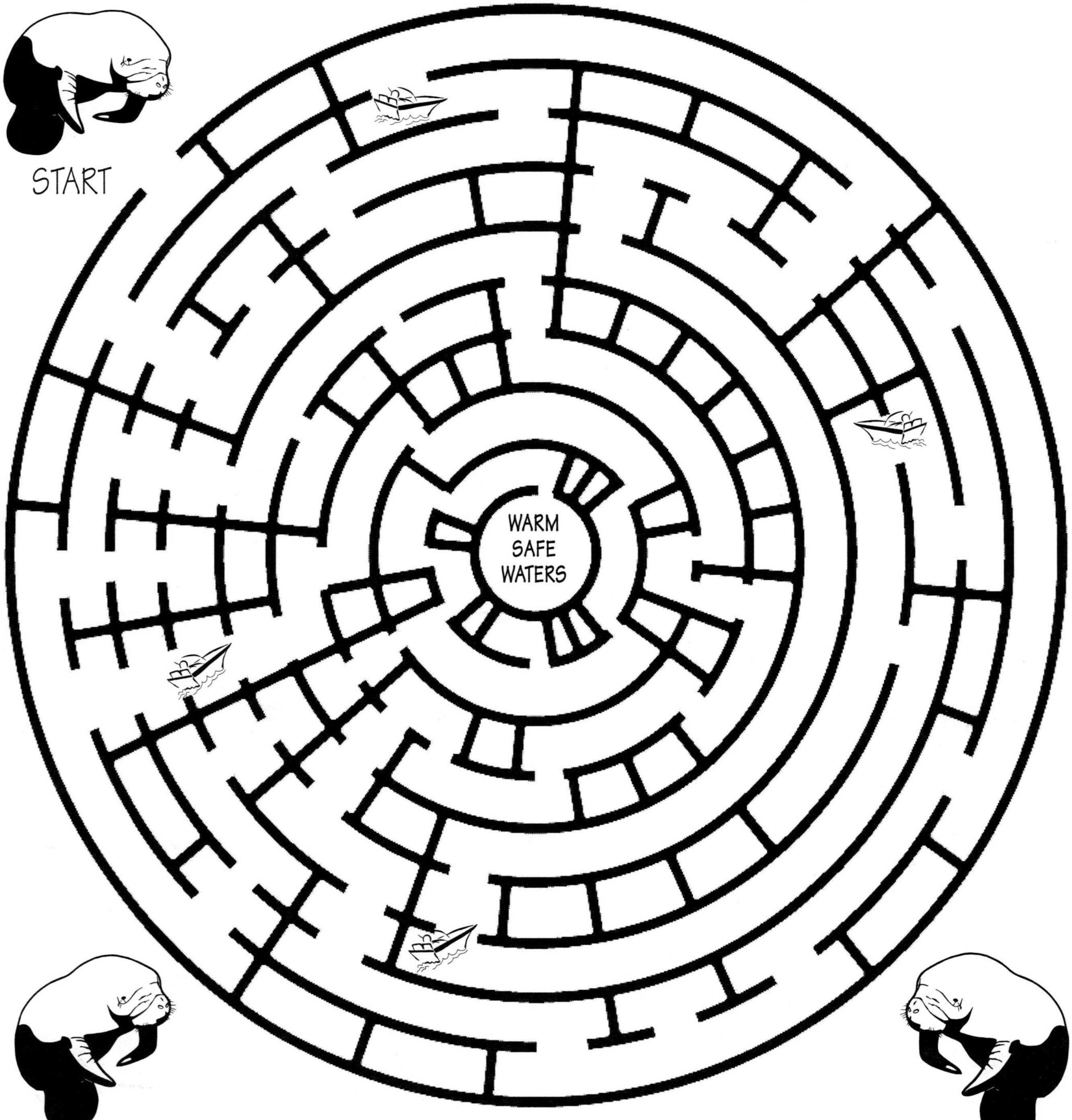

Howling Hurricanes

Word Search

A hurricane is a violent storm with wind speeds more than 74 miles (119 kilometers) per hour.

FIND THE NAMES OF HURRICANES THAT HAVE BLOWN THROUGH OR NEAR THE COAST OF FLORIDA.

ANDREW	HUGO	GORDON	OPAL
GEORGES	MITCH	EARL	LILI
FRANCES	ALLISON	ERIN	BERTHA
EMILY	GRACE	BONNIE	AGNES

F R A N C E S B F L
A G N E S M I T C H
T H D J I H R E M T
L U R E V U R U M X
U G E O R G E S Y A
Q O W P Z O A E X L
W R V A C Z R M W L
Z D L L B A L I L I
B O N N I E D L E S
F N G R A C E Y R O
B E R T H A E R I N

Color Me!
Brown
Like the Ocala thoroughbred horses
Brown
BLUE
Like the ocean
Blue
YELLOW
The Sunshine State
Yellow
RED
Like Florida's ruby red grapefruit.
Red
Black
BLACK
Like the Cannons at Castillo de San Marcos.
Purple
PURPLE
Like Florida's wildflowers.
Green
GREEN
Like Florida's lush forests.
Orange
ORANGE
Like the fruit.
FLORIDA

Endangered and Threatened Florida

"Endangered" and "threatened" means an animal population has declined so low that they could cease to exist in the world. When a certain type of animal reaches this point, they are placed on an endangered or threatened species list by the federal government. After being placed on this list, the animals are kept safe from hunters or anything that would disturb their homes.

Florida has many animals on the endangered or threatened species list, including the Florida panther, the Florida black bear, the Big Cypress fox squirrel, river otter, wood stork, American kestrel, snail kite, bald eagle, Florida grasshopper sparrow, American alligator, eastern indigo snake, and striped mud turtle.

Can you help rescue these endangered and threatened animals by unscrambling their names below?

oowd kstro ________ ________

esanret digino knsae ________ ________ ________

lofdair npaethr ________ ________

lofdair balkc aber ________ ________ ________

gib ypcsres ________ ________

xfo qrsuleri ________ ________

maircena llgatiaro ________ ________

vrrei toetr ________ ________

ANSWERS: wood stork, eastern indigo snake, Florida panther, Florida black bear, Big Cypress fox squirrel, American alligator, river otter

Pirates of Florida

Pirate "Old John" Gomez, the former cabin boy of notorious pirate José Gaspar, once escaped hanging by swimming to the pirate's den on Gasparilla Island at Boca Grande. Captured as a teenager by Gaspar, recruited pirate Gomez also tried his hand as an Indian fighter, woodsman, farmer, fisherman, and ship's pilot during the Civil War. (Very) Old John eventually settled on Panther Key, now called Gomez Key, and lived contentedly until he accidentally drowned at the age of 122!

Color the Treasure Chest:

Woodgrain=brown,

Trim=yellow,

Round Jewels=blue and green.

Add all the booty (treasure) inside that you want!

Something Fishy Here!

The *istiophorus platypterus*, or sailfish, is Florida's state saltwater fish. It can swim as fast as 60 miles (100 kilometers) per hour! Sailfishing is one of Florida's most popular sports.
When a sailfish is hooked, it thrashes violently trying to get itself free from the fisherman's hook.

There's something fishy about the picture below! Part of the picture is missing.

Draw what is going on above the water line (a boat, fishermen, etc.) and add some other underwater fish friends.

What Does Florida Mean To You?

F is for Fun in the sun!

L is for Lush Landscapes!

O is for all the Oranges grown!

R is for Rainy days!

I is for the many Islands!

D is for Dolphins at play!

A is for all the Alligators!

Now write the name of your town, and then come up with descriptive words to represent each letter.

Our Cities, Our Towns

Florida has a wide variety of cities and towns. Historic St. Augustine is known as the oldest European city in America. Orlando, located in Central Florida, is a hub for amusement park visitors seeking thrills and excitement. Home to the famous Daytona International Speedway, Daytona Beach offers visitors some of the world's whitest beaches. At Cape Canaveral, many spacecraft have been launched, including *Apollo II,* which landed the first men on the moon. Panama City, a popular resort for sun seeking travelers, has close to 100 percent quartz sand on its beaches. Miami, in South Florida, is a haven for Cuban immigrants, especially in Little Havana. Key West is known as the southernmost town in the Continental United States. Palm Beach, in southeastern Florida, is an area known for its wealthy visitors. All in all, Florida has much more than its famous sunshine to offer its visitors and natives!

Match the city with something that it is known for:

1. _____ Cape Canaveral
2. _____ St. Augustine
3. _____ Miami
4. _____ Key West
5. _____ Orlando
6. _____ Panama City
7. _____ Palm Beach
8. _____ Daytona Beach

A. oldest European town in U.S.

B. beaches made from almost 100 percent quartz sand

C. wealthy visitors

D. mecca for racing fans

E. city with a Cuban flair

F. known for its many amusement parks

G. southernmost town in Continental U.S.

H. launching pad for space shuttles

ANSWERS: 1.H, 2.A, 3.E, 4.G, 5.F, 6.B, 7.C, 8.D

Map of North America

This is a map of North America. Florida is one of the 50 states in the United States.

Color the state of Florida red.

Color the rest of the United States yellow. Alaska and Hawaii are part of the United States and should also be colored yellow.

Color Canada green. Color Mexico blue.

The Reclusive Florida Panther

In 1982, students in Florida voted the Florida Panther as our state animal. Very few Florida Panthers are around these days because they are the state's most endangered animal. However, some still live in the Everglades National Park. Most Floridians will never see the panthers because they tend to stay away from people whenever possible. Panthers grow to almost 8 feet (2.4 meters) long and can weigh as much as 125 pounds (56.25 kilograms). They have tawny brown coats, and have tails that hang so low that they almost drag the ground!

Arrange these descriptive words below using the Word List.

WORD BANK

national
tawny
feet
Everglades
panther
yikes

1. _ _ (_) _ y
2. _ e _ (_)
3. _ a _ (_) _ _ _
4. _ _ (_) _ g _ _ _ _ _ _
5. (_) _ t _ _ _ _ _ _
6. (_) _ _ _ _ s

Now unscramble the "bubble" letters to discover the mystery word in the sentence below:

Florida Panthers can leap up to _ _ _ _ _ _ feet!

ANSWERS: 1. tawny, 2. feet, panther, Everglades, national, yikes, Mystery word: twenty

Florida Cities

Circle Tallahassee in red. It is our state's capital. The star is the map symbol for our capital.
Circle Miami in yellow. It is close to the Everglades.
Circle St. Augustine in blue. It is close to the Atlantic Ocean.
Circle Pensacola in brown. It is close to the Gulf of Mexico.
Circle Cape Canaveral in orange. It is home of the Kennedy Space Center.
Add your city or town to the map if it's not here. Circle it in green. Give it a ☺ symbol to show where you live there.

Oops! The compass rose is missing its cardinal directions.

Write N S E W on the compass rose.

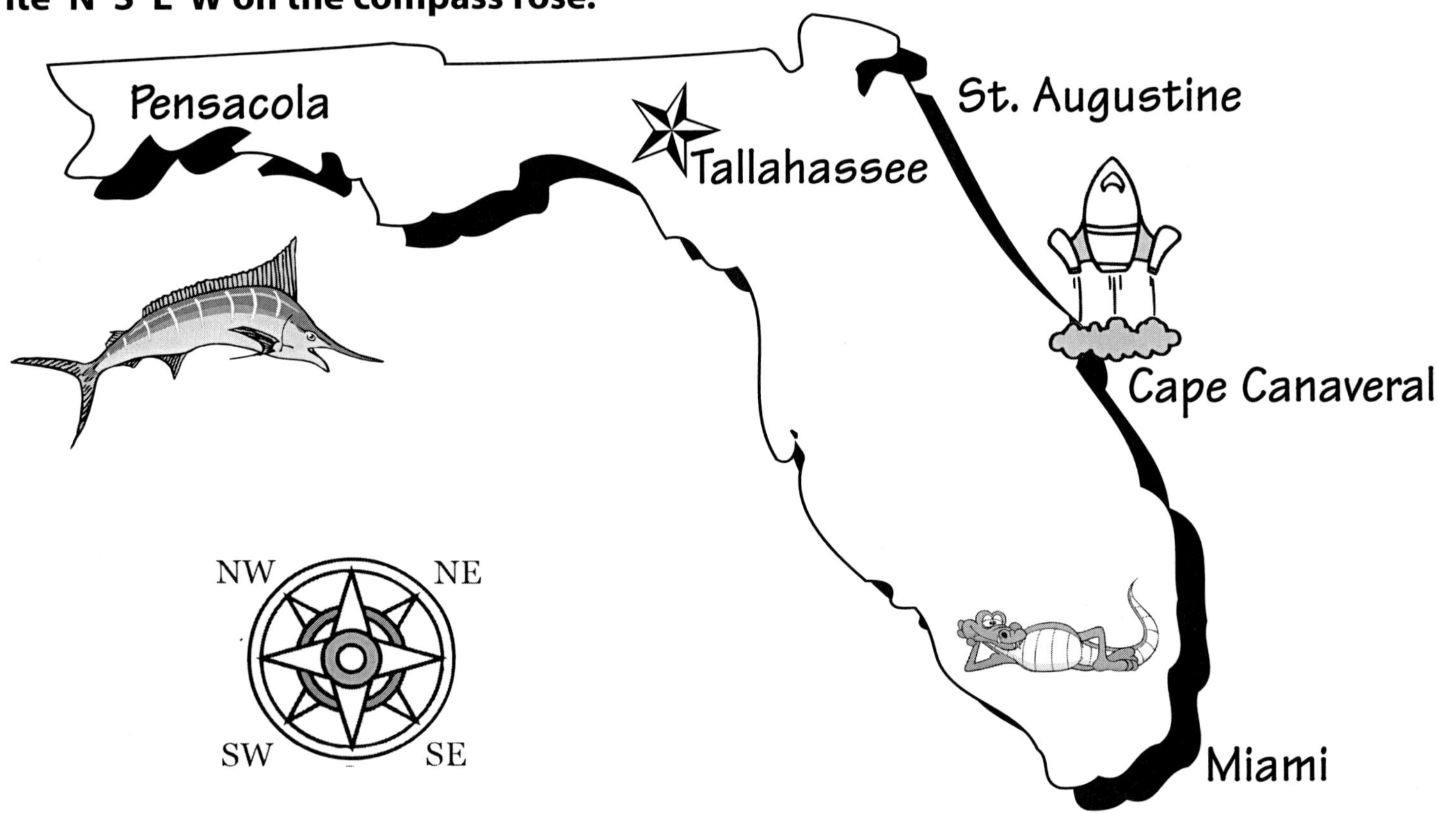

Meet Fred the Fisherman!

Fred is a fisherman from Jacksonville. He fishes in the St. Johns River. His father and grandfather taught him how to fish. Fred fishes for bass, bluegill, and crappie.

Help Fred reach the good fishing waters.

Spongy Jumping

One of the world's largest suppliers of natural sponges is Tarpon Springs. Greek immigrants arrived as early as the 1900s to dive for sponges. Today, divers bring sponges to the surface in baskets. Once on the deck of the boat, the sponges are bruised by walking on them and then are allowed to decay. The skeleton is cleaned and then dried for shipment. Today, Tarpan Springs is still mostly Greek and abounds with sponge-fishing traditions and lore.

Dive in the water below and count the sponges. I found ☐

ANSWER: 13

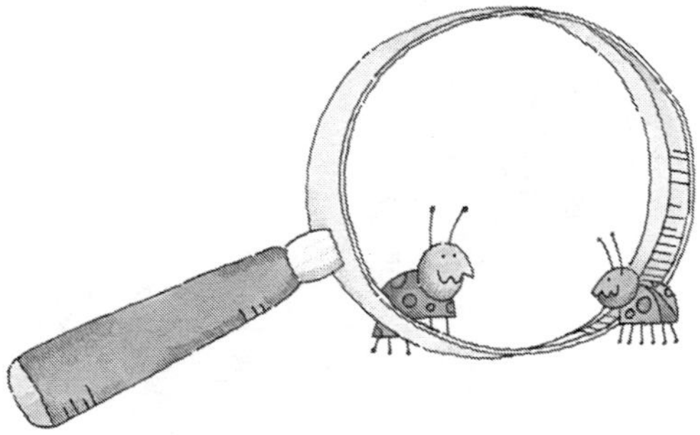

Searching For Sammy Shrimp

Florida shrimpers supply over 10% of the shrimp for America each year. Although the shrimp may seem plentiful when you go to your favorite seafood restaurants, they are actually getting more difficult to find each year. With more shrimpers competing to catch shrimp, the numbers of mature shrimp are dwindling. Other factors, such as water pollution and parasites, can cause the number of shrimp to decline. Some years there are so few shrimp to be caught that many shrimpers decide to look for other jobs.

See if you can find all the delicious shrimp dishes below.

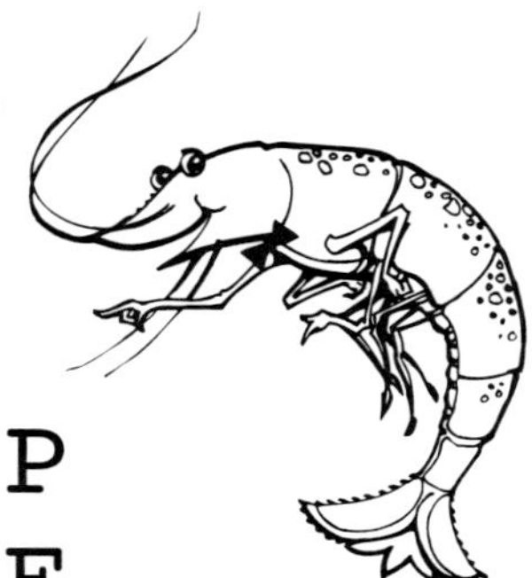

CREOLE
POPCORN
BUTTERFLY
COCKTAIL
FRIED
SCAMPI
GRILLED
BROILED
TEMPURA
CAJUN
SALAD

S	B	R	O	I	L	E	D	P
F	U	T	E	C	P	C	S	E
G	T	E	K	R	S	O	C	T
K	T	M	V	E	A	C	A	C
D	E	P	G	O	L	K	M	K
W	R	U	R	L	A	T	P	L
O	F	R	I	E	D	A	I	R
K	L	A	L	Q	R	I	S	D
Q	Y	M	L	N	T	L	C	S
X	V	Y	E	L	D	I	A	C
I	T	F	D	A	T	C	J	A
L	R	S	C	A	P	V	U	R
N	P	O	P	C	O	R	N	Y

Our State's Rules

Use the code to complete the sentences.

A	B	C	D	E	F	G	H	I	J	K	L	M	N	O	P	Q	R	S	T
1	2	3	4	5	6	7	8	9	10	11	12	13	14	15	16	17	18	19	20

U	V	W	X	Y	Z
21	22	23	24	25	26

---

1. State rules are called ___ ___ ___ ___.
   12 1 23 19

2. Laws are made in our state ___ ___ ___ ___ ___ ___ ___.
   3 1 16 9 20 1 12

3. The leader of our state is the ___ ___ ___ ___ ___ ___ ___ ___.
   7 15 22 5 18 14 15 18

4. We live in the state of ___ ___ ___ ___ ___ ___ ___.
   6 12 15 18 9 4 1

5. The capital of our state is ___ ___ ___ ___ ___ ___ ___ ___ ___ ___ ___.
   20 1 12 12 1 8 1 19 19 5 5

FLORIDA!!!

ANSWERS: 1.laws 2.capital 3.governor 4.Florida 5.Tallahassee

Shipwrecked!

The Florida coast is littered with Spanish treasure ships with cargos of gold, silver bars, and coins. The earliest known shipwreck in Florida lies at the bottom of the ocean on Florida's Gulf Coast, just off Emanuel Point in Pensacola Bay. Sometimes, after a bad storm at sea, coins wash up on the beach to be found by beachcombers. The town of Key West was founded in 1828 due to the misfortune of shipping merchants. These wreckers, as they were known, took advantage of the many shipwrecks that happened on the reefs. Today, treasure hunting is a serious business in the Keys and around the Florida coastline.

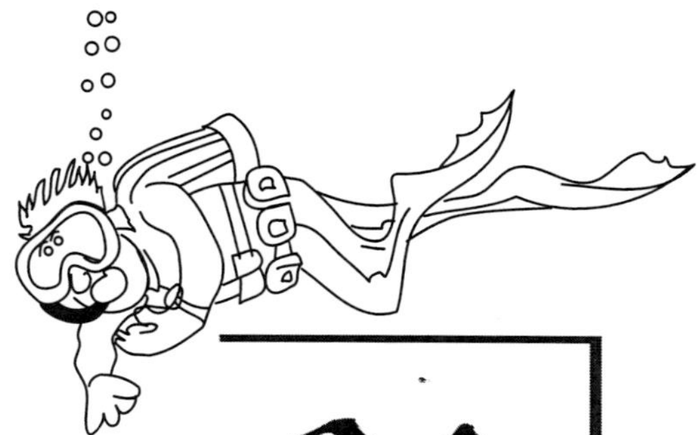

Help this treasure hunter find the gold coins.

Do You Know These Floridians?

From the Word Bank, find my name and fill in the blank. (My name might be used twice.)

WORD BANK

John D. Pennekamp
Christina Meacham
Osceola
Lue Gim Gong
Harriet Beecher Stowe
Ruth Bryan Owen
Zachary Taylor
Vincente Ybor

I was a Seminole Indian chief who violently opposed moving my people from their land.
Who am I? ______________________________

I was the first Congresswoman from the Deep South who represented Florida in the U.S. House of Representatives.
Who am I? ______________________________

I was a white woman activist who spent most of my life working to help African-Americans. I wrote *Uncle Tom's Cabin*.
Who am I? ______________________________

I was a Cuban industrialist who established the cigar making industry in the U.S.
Who am I? ______________________________

I was the first African-American woman principal of a Tampa school.
Who am I? ______________________________

I was a horticulturist who developed the late ripening, frost resistant orange.
Who am I? ______________________________

I was editor of the *Miami Herald*. My conservation efforts led to the creation of Everglades National Park.
Who am I? ______________________________

I was a military leader who became the twelfth President of the United States.
Who am I? ______________________________

ANSWERS: Osceola, Ruth Bryan Owen, Harriet Beecher Stowe, Vincente Ybor, Christina Meacham, Lue Gim Gong, John D. Pennekamp, Zachary Taylor

Time Travel

Take yourself back in time...
It is February, 1595. You are sitting on top of a high flat-top fence post. As you survey your surroundings, you see hundreds of these tall fence posts in a huge circle. Inside is a circular village with 30 or 40 cone shaped huts. The roofs are made of thatched palm branches and the walls of woven vines. You have never seen anything like it before. Looking behind you in the distance, you see Fort Caroline. As you watch, tall men with their hair in a topknot and wearing animal skins, enter the village with shellfish they caught in the St. Johns River. They hand the catch to women with black hair hanging freely and dressed in Spanish Moss clothing. You can see that many men have tattoos, and you see what is surely a chief. His mouth is encircled with blue tattoos. You are watching life among the Timucuans. They are Indians who lived in Florida for about 1,000 years. Now stand up, dust yourself off, and come back to the future. Isn't it good to be home?!

Match the following:

1. What type of people are these? ______________________
2. Where did they get some of their food? ______________________
3. What is the name of the tribe? ______________________
4. What is the shape of the village? ______________________

A. Square
B. Marshalls
C. St. Johns River
D. Circular
E. Italians
F. Timucuans
G. A well
H. Indians

Answers: 1.H 2.C 3.F 4.D

Marvelous Marjorie!

An adopted Floridian, Marjorie Kinnan Rawlings was a writer who lived on a farm in central Florida, near Ocala National Forest. Much of what she wrote described early settlers in Florida and the lives they led. Perhaps her best known novel was *The Yearling*. Winning a Pulitzer Prize in 1939, *The Yearling* was later made into a movie. Not only did she write about the natural beauty of Florida and its people, Rawlings was also a hunter and fisherwoman. In her later years she became an advocate for rural life in central Florida.

The Yearling is about a young boy living in the Florida wilderness with his parents and his pet deer.

Write an adventure story about a pet you have had or would like to have.

Electrifying

On a hot summer night in Florida, you might see this flash across the sky. Florida is the lightning capital of the USA. We get more lightning strikes than any other state! Florida even has its own "lightning belt" which is an area stretching from Orlando and Tampa, south along the west coast to Fort Myers, and east to Lake Okeechobee. One study showed 120 days of thunderstorms occurred in one year within a 50-mile (31.25 kilometers) area of Tampa. Now, that's electrifying!

Color the  **space yellow.** **Color the**  **space dark blue.**

Please Come to Florida!

You have a friend who lives in Florida. She is thinking of moving to Florida because she has heard that there are a lot of jobs in the tourist industry. You want to encourage your friend to come to Florida.

Write her a letter describing Florida and some of the employment opportunities.

Florida is home to the largest of all family resorts, Walt Disney World. Florida also offers many other opportunities for exciting adventure. Many are educational, such as the Kennedy Space Center in Cape Canaveral.

Operation Conservation!

With over-development of its land and continued ravaging of its forests, Florida's natural landscape is slowly being eaten away, one bite at a time. Farms and grazing land have taken the place of once abundant prairies. Half of the freshwater marshes in southwestern Florida have been drained. From 1982 to 1992, the forestland in Florida decreased 27% while the developed land grew by 35%. Even Florida's Everglades cannot escape harm. Fertilizers and wastes feeding into its water from neighboring communities are poisoning and killing many land and water animals. Also, there are two different groups who look at the Everglades in two different ways. One group wants to use and develop the land while the other group wants to preserve it.
Where do you stand on issues facing Florida's Everglades?

Look at the two columns below. Try to write three reasons under each column to support each cause.

Developers	**Preservationists**
______________________	______________________
______________________	______________________
______________________	______________________

Now that you have looked at both viewpoints, which group would you support in the future?
Why do you feel this way? ______________________________

____

____

____

Florida's Venomous Snakes!

Only six species of venomous (poisonous) snakes live in Florida.
Using the alphabet code, see if you can find out their names.

Use the code to complete the sentences.

A	B	C	D	E	F	G	H	I	J	K	L	M	N	O	P	Q	R	S	T
1	2	3	4	5	6	7	8	9	10	11	12	13	14	15	16	17	18	19	20

U	V	W	X	Y	Z
21	22	23	24	25	26

RATTLESNAKES

___ ___ ___ ___ ___ ___ ___ ___ ___ ___ ___
4 9 1 13 15 14 4 2 1 3 11

___ ___ ___ ___ ___ ___ ___ ___ ___　　___ ___ ___ ___ ___
3 1 14 5 2 18 1 11 5　　16 25 7 13 25

OTHER SNAKES

___ ___ ___ ___ ___　　___ ___ ___ ___ ___ ___ ___ ___
23 1 20 5 18　　13 15 3 3 1 19 9 14

___ ___ ___ ___ ___ ___ ___ ___ ___ ___
3 15 16 16 5 18 8 5 1 4

___ ___ ___ ___ ___　　___ ___ ___ ___ ___
3 15 18 1 12　　19 14 1 11 5

ANSWERS: Diamondback, canebrake pygmy, water moccasin, copperhead, coral snake

A Key To The Keys

The Florida Keys are a thin string of islands that begin at Key Largo and continue westward more than 100 miles along highway U.S.1 to Key West. Separated into two sections, the Upper and Lower Keys, they were once part of a large coral reef almost 100,000 years ago.

Check the following that are true about the Keys:

_____ The Keys attract treasure hunters
_____ Key West is the last stop on the Overseas Highway
_____ An early Spanish explorer named the Keys Los Martires
_____ Purple Island was named for its violet colored snails
_____ John Pennekamp Coral Reef is an underwater park

I hope you said all were true, because they are! Now, answer the following questions about Florida's fabulous keys:

1. The biggest of the Key islands is ________ ______________.
2. ____________ _____________ or Cow Key, is where the manatee play.
3. The "deep bay" is called _______________ _______________ .
4. ___________ _____________ is where John James Audubon wrote about natural wonders of the island.
5. ______________ ______________ is where construction of the Seven Mile Bridge began.

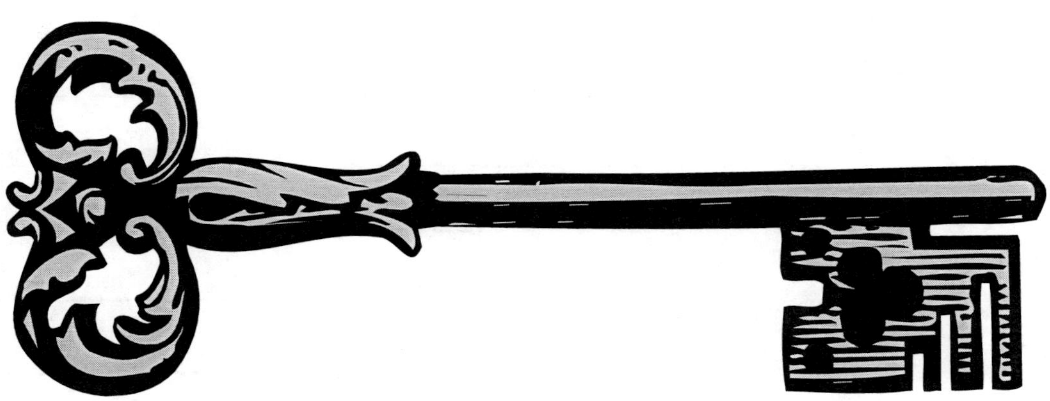

ANSWERS: 1. Key Largo 2. Key Vaca 3. Bahia Honda 4. Indian Key 5. Long Key

Florida in the Civil War

Florida was split during the Civil War with about 15,000 Floridians joining the Confederate troops, while only about 2,000 Floridians joined the Union Army. During this time, Florida's prized cattle were used to feed the hungry Confederate Army. A special "cow protectors" batallion known as the Cracker Cowhunters was formed to insure the supply of cattle. Florida also supplied the Confederate Army with cotton, pork, fish, salt, and vegetables. The only major battle fought in Florida during the Civil War was at Olustee, on February 20, 1864, near Lake City.

Pretend it is February 19,1864, and you are camped out near Olustee. There is a rumor that a battle is going to take place in the morning. Write a letter to a friend telling the reasons why this war is being fought.

A River Runs Through It!

The state of Florida is "flooded" with many rivers. See if you can wade right in and figure out which river name completes the sentences below!

1. If you're doing laundry, you wouldn't want to wash your clothes in the

   __ __ __ __ __ __ __ __ __ __ River!

2. Hungry? Don't plan on catching anything for supper in

   __ __ __ __ __ __ __ __ __ __ Creek!

3. If you like swimming with the manatees, you might like to swim here a "little" bit better. It's the __ __ __ __ __ __ __ __ __ __ __ __ __ River!

4. Looking for a quiet place to rest? You might find it near the __ __ __ __ __ River!

5. If you're searching for a little bit of heaven on earth, you might try one of these three rivers: __ __ __ __ __ __ __, __ __ __ __ __ __ __, or __ __ __ __ __ __ __!

6. If you need to color a rainbow, you may wish to visit the __ __ __ __ __ __ River!

7. You'll be swimming the state song, if you swim in the __ __ __ __ __ __ __ __ River!

8. If you don't want to go in over your head, you might want to dip in the

   __ __ __ __ __ River!

ANSWERS: 1. Blackwater, 2. Fisheating, 3. Little Manatee, 4. Peace, 5. St. Johns, St. Marks, St. Marys 6. Yellow, 7. Suwannee, 8. Shoal.

Slavery In Florida

Almost 50% of the population of Florida in 1840 were slaves. In 1845, Florida became the 27th state in the country and was admitted as a slave state. Since the majority of slaves were owned by the plantation owners, only about 33% of white Floridians owned slaves. Some slaves were treated harshly, especially those who worked on sugar cane plantations during the sugar-boiling season and those on the cotton plantations during harvesting season. At these times, it wasn't uncommon to work all day in the broiling sun and then half the night. Other slaves were loved as family members. One such slave who was brought to Florida in the 1830s worked for a family in Tallahassee. When she died in 1858, it was said that the family lost their second mother.

She was known as this "faithful servant," and given a special name. To find out what her name was, cross out every other letter. The first two have been done for you. The letters that are left over will spell her name.

M ~~U~~ A ~~A~~ U T M S A E M H O T L U L O I K E

M A ___ ___ ___   ___ ___ ___ ___ ___ ___

ANSWER: Mauma Mollie

The Seven Mile Bridge

When industrialist Henry Flagler set his sights on the construction of the Seven Mile Bridge, he was already 75 years old. Although it took five years to build and was the most expensive bridge in the railway system, "The Railway That Went To Sea" finally connected to Key West in January 1912. In 1936, the state of Florida began converting the defunct railway into the Overseas Highway. At this time the bridge was widened from 14 (4.27 meters) to 22 feet (6.71 meters). It was open for service until 1982, when a higher, wider, more modern bridge was built. With the inclusion of its approaches, the world's largest segmented bridge actually spans 9 miles (14.4 kilometers) from Knights Key to Bahia Honda.

Answer the following math questions about the reading selection.

WORK AREA

1. If Flagler was 75 years old at the beginning of construction, how old was he when it was completed? _______ years old

2. The railway bridge was opened in 1912. In 1936, the state of Florida began converting the bridge to the Overseas Highway. How many years was the railway bridge in operation? _______ years

3. The Overseas Highway was widened from 14 feet to 22 feet. How many feet was it widened? ______ feet

4. When a new, improved bridge was opened in 1982, how many years had it been since the Overseas Highway last reconstruction? _______ y

5. How many miles do the approaches of the bridge add to its total length? _______ miles

BONUS: How many times were mathematical numbers or words used in the reading selection? _______ times

ANSWERS: 1. 80 years old, 2. 24 years, 3. 8 feet, 4. 46 years, 5. 2 miles, BONUS: 12 times

Design your own Diamante on Florida!

A *diamante* is a cool diamond-shaped poem on any subject. You can write your very own diamante poem on Florida below by following the simple line by line directions. Give it a try!

Line 1: Write the name of your state.

Line 2: Write the names of two animals native to your state.

Line 3: Write the names of three of your state's important cities.

Line 4: Write the names of four of your state's important industries or agricultural products.

Line 5: Write the names of your state bird, the state flower, and state tree.

Line 6: Write the names of two of your state's geographical features.

Line 7: Our state nickname is the __________ State.

____

______________ ______________

______________ ______________ ______________

______________ ______________ ______________ ______________

______________ ______________ ______________

______________ ______________

____

Florida Word Wheel

From the Word Wheel of Florida names, answer the following questions.

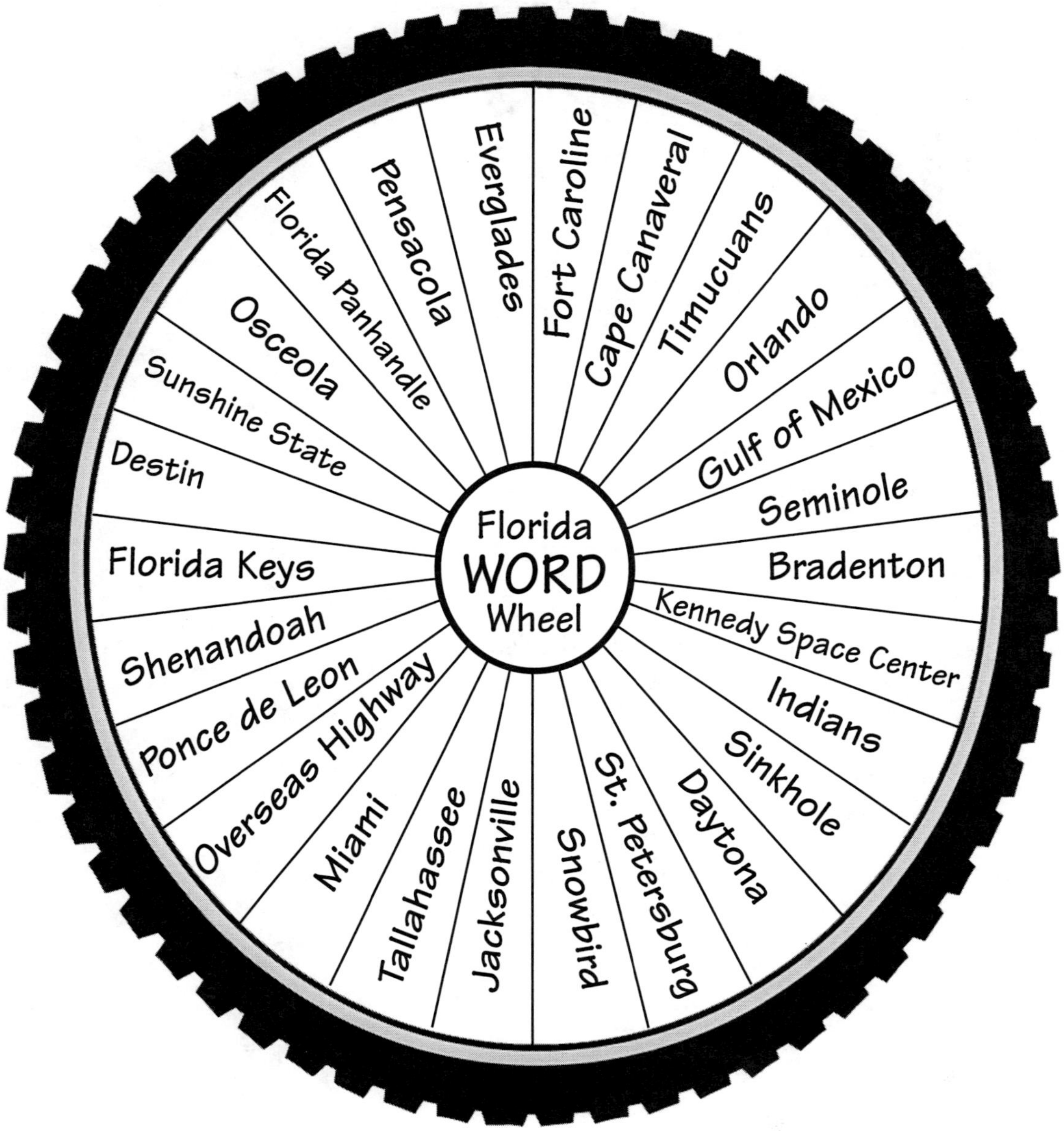

1. The capital of Florida is ____________________________.
2. Some very famous amusement parks occupy a large portion of the city of _________________.
3. The first people to live in Florida were ____________________.
4. Florida's nickname is the ________________________ _______________.
5. A long bridge-tunnel that connects the mainland to Key Largo and is 100 miles long is the __________________________________.
6. The _______________________________ are Florida's most distinctive wetlands.
7. A group of islands off the southern tip of Florida are called the ________________________.
8. A hole or water-filled pit that "wasn't there yesterday" is called a ________________________.
9. ______________________ was the great leader of Florida's Seminole Indians.

ANSWERS: 1. Tallahasse 2. Orlando 3. Indians 4. Sunshine State 5. Overseas Highway 6. Everglades
7. Florida Keys 8. sinkhole 9. Osceola

Rhymin' Riddles

I was launched from Canaveral, nicknamed "Snake Chaser".
Through the wilderness I zoomed as quick as a racer.

What am I? ____________________

Cross the Everglades by boat, or do it by car;
If by car, use me, I'm covered with tar.

What am I? ____________________ ____________________

Florida has more courses to play me than any other state;
So pick up your putter and let's make a date.

What am I? ____________________

If you hear twin sonic booms, look up where you're standing;
It's the sound that I make coming in for a landing.

What am I? ____________________ ____________________

About 500 of me appear each year;
I'm openings in the ground so be careful, dear!

What am I? ____________________

ANSWERS: Rocket, Alligator Alley (Tamiami Trail), Golf, Space Shuttle, Sinkholes

Early Native Americans Abound!

The first people ever to reach the land that would one day become the state of Florida descended from Eurasians who had crossed a frozen bridge from Siberia to Alaska. This continent to continent walk may have taken place as many as 12,000 years ago.

See if you can match their smarts by completing the match below!

_____ 1.	Coastal Indians	A.	used wooden spears with stone points
_____ 2.	for use during winter	B.	corn, beans, and squash
_____ 3.	named Tallahassee	C.	5,000 year old settlement
_____ 4.	made pottery	D.	dried and smoked game
_____ 5.	crops grown	E.	occupied the most fertile land in North Florida
_____ 6.	Seminoles	F.	800 years before any other American people
_____ 7.	hunters	G.	fished and gathered shellfish
_____ 8.	Little Salt Spring	H.	means "old town"

Answers: 1.G, 2.D, 3.H, 4.F, 5.B, 6.E, 7.A, 8.C

The Mighty Suwannee River

The most famous river in Florida is the Suwannee River. Rising 120 feet (37 meters) above sea level, the Suwannee bubbles out of the Okefenokee Swamp near the Georgia-Florida border. Winding west to east, then taking a southwesterly course, the Suwannee travels 266 miles (428 kilometers) through eight Florida counties. The Suwannee River is even mentioned in our state song!

Answer the following questions by filling in the blanks below.

1. The Suwannee takes what final direction as it travels 266 miles? S _ _ _ _ _ _ _ _ _ _ _ _

2. The most famous river in Florida is _ U _ _ _ _ _ _

3. The Suwannee River begins flowing in what direction? W _ _ _

4. "Old Folks at Home" became the what of Florida? _ _ A _ _   _ _ _ _

5. Stephen Foster spelled the Suwannee how? _ _ _ N _ _

6. The Suwannee travels throughout eight what? _ _ _ N _ _ _ _

7. The Suwannee begins at what swamp? _ _ E _ _ _ _ _ _ _

8. What state borders the Suwannee at its beginning? _ E _ _ _ _ _

Answers: 1. SOUTHWESTERLY, 2. SUWANNEE, 3. WEST, 4. STATE SONG, 5. SWANEE, 6. COUNTIES, 7. OKEFENOKEE, 8. GEORGIA

Ships Come Sailing!

In 1539, Spanish conquistador, Hernando De Soto sailed into Tampa Bay, landing near the present-day city of Bradenton. Looking for gold-filled cities, de Soto and his crew were soon disheartened when they found only wilderness and hostile Indians. Many times the Spaniards would awaken to find one of their members hanging headless by his limbs from a nearby tree. Discouraged, De Soto and his explorers pushed north completely out of Florida.

Color De Soto's ship.

Civil Rights For All

Florida was important in America's civil rights movement. One of the leaders in the state was labor leader A. Philip Randolph. Born in Crescent City, Randolph helped organize black workers into unions, or groups that worked for better working conditions for their members. When Randolph was 74, he was behind the most famous civil rights march in American history. The year was 1963, and over 200,000 people came to hear Dr. Martin Luther King, Jr. make his "I Have a Dream" speech. Dr. King's dream was equal rights for all Americans. He worked very hard to make African-Americans "free at last".

Many other African-Americans made significant accomplishments for the state of Florida, the nation, and in some cases, the world.

Try matching their accomplishments with their names.

_____ 1. Dwight Gooden

_____ 2. James Weldon Johnson

_____ 3. Sidney Poitier

_____ 4. Julian Adderly

_____ 5. Mary McLeod Bethune

_____ 6. Daniel James, Jr.

_____ 7. Artis Gilmore

_____ 8. Robert Meacham

_____ 9. Mary Singleton

_____ 10. Joseph W. Hatchett

A. Actor who won 1963 Academy Award for *Lillies of The Field*

B. has one of the highest shooting percentages in NBA history

C. wrote the black national anthem "Lift Every Voice and Sing"

D. educator who opened a school in Daytona Beach

E. 1984 National League Rookie of the year

F. helped establish Florida's public education system

G. city councilwoman and state legislator

H. great jazz saxophonist

I. first African-American four star general

J. Florida's first African-American Supreme Court Justice

ANSWERS: 1.E, 2.C, 3.A, 4.H, 5.D, 6.I, 7.B, 8.F, 9.G, 10.J

Come Join Us In The Circus

Help Wanted

The Flying High Circus at Florida State University is seeking responsible, fun-loving students to join our full 3-ring circus on campus. You must be enrolled at Florida State University and be willing to cooperate with other circus members, learn new skills, and perform in public.

Let us know why you would or would not make a good member of our circus. Write your comments below.

Florida Wheel of Fortune, Indian Style!

The names of Florida's many Indian tribes contain enough consonants to play … Wheel of Fortune!

See if you can figure out the Wheel of Fortune-style puzzles below! "Vanna" has given you some consonants in each word to help you out.

[ ] [ ] [S]

[ ] [P] [ ] [L] [ ] [ ] [ ] [ ] [ ]

[ ] [ ] [L] [ ] [S] [ ]

[T] [ ] [Q] [ ] [ ] [ ] [ ] [ ]

[ ] [ ] [M] [ ] [C] [ ] [ ]

[S] [ ] [ ] [ ] [ ] [ ] [L] [ ]

ANSWERS: AIS, APALACHEE, CALUSA, TEQUESTA, TIMUCUA, SEMINOLE

Florida Writers

Fill in the missing first or last name of these famous Florida writers.

1. First name: Ernest
   Last name: ____________________

2. First name: ____________________
   Last name: Bartram

3. First name: Archie
   Last name: ____________________

4. First name: __________ Stoneman
   Last name: Douglas

5. First name: James
   Last name: ____________________

6. First name: ____________________
   Last name: MacDonald

7. First name: Sidney
   Last name: ____________________

Answers: 1.Hemingway 2.William 3.Carp 4.Marjory 5.Johnson 6.John 7.Lanier

Geographic Tools

Part 1: Beside each task you need to accomplish, put the initials of the tool that can best help you!

(CR) Compass Rose
(M) Map
(K) Map key/legend
(LL) Longitude and Latitude
(G) Grid

1. ______ I need to find the geographic location of Germany.
2. ______ I need to find where an airport is located near Orlando.
3. ______ I need to find which way is north.
4. ______ I need to chart a route from Florida to California.
5. ______ I need to find a small Florida town on a map.

Part 2: Match the items on the left with the items on the right.

1. Grid system
2. Compass rose
3. Longitude and latitude
4. Two of Florida's borders
5. Symbols on a map

A. Map key or legend
B. Georgia and Alabama
C. A system of letters and numbers
D. Imaginary lines around the earth
E. Shows N, S, E, and W

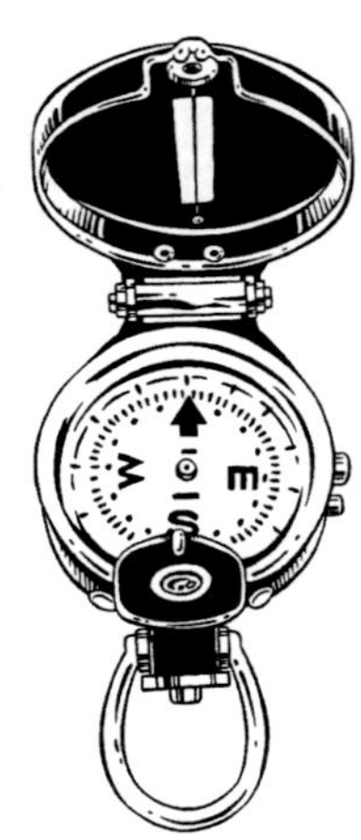

ANSWERS: Part 1: 1.LL 2.K 3.CR 4.M 5.G Part 2: 1.C 2.E 3.D 4.B 5.A

Snail Shells

The Florida tree snails eat fungi that grow on the sides of tropical trees. They scrape the fungi off so completely that they leave a trail on the trunks. The snail shells range in color from white to yellow and have multi-colored stripes of pink, yellow, green, and white.

Color the Florida tree snail. Don't forget to add the many stripes on the snail shell.

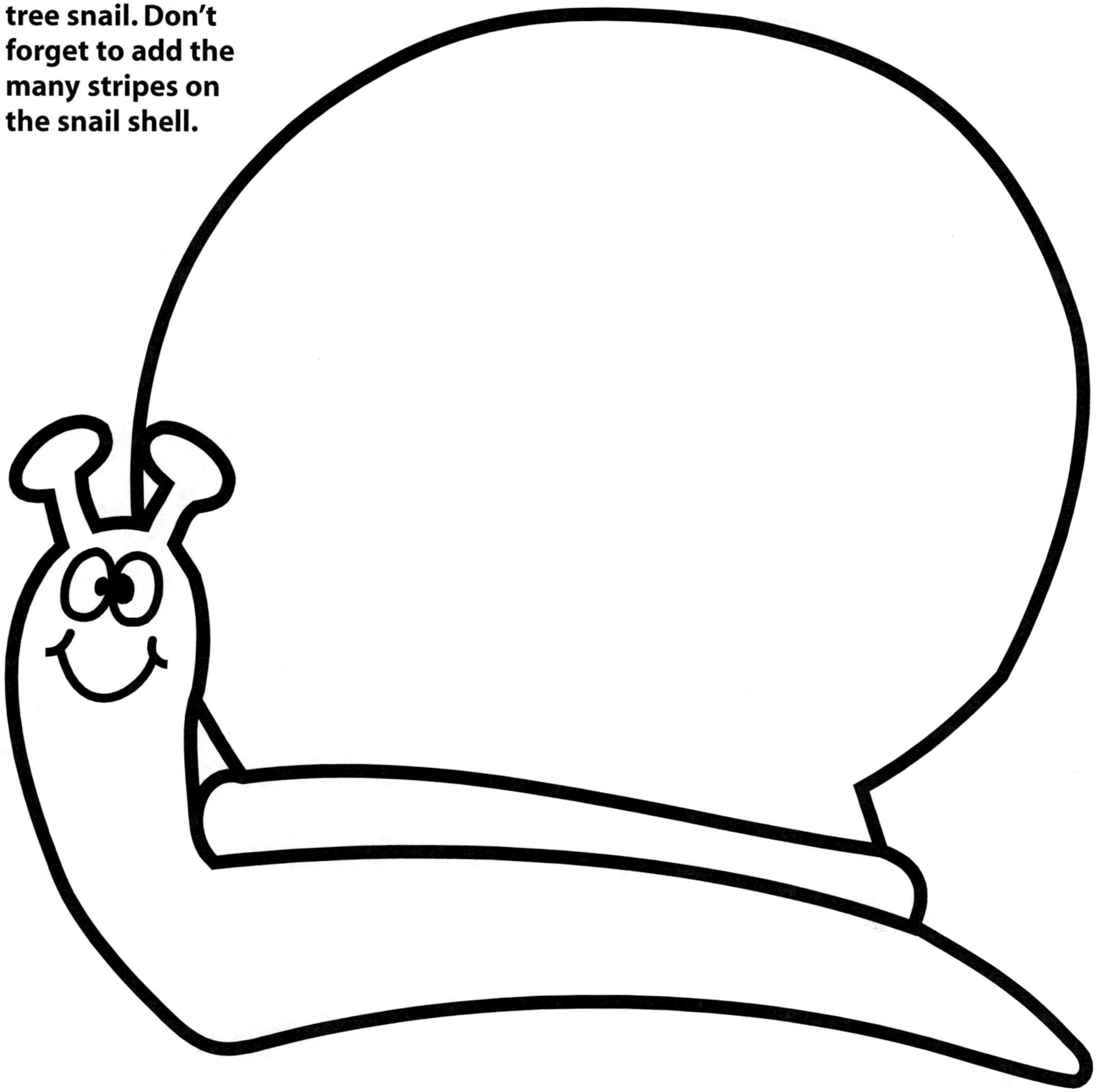

Florida's Fury

The landscape of Florida with its gentle breezes and white beaches often hide the natural disasters that at times strike our state.

See if you can uncover some of the natural disasters that affect the state of Florida. Use the Word Bank below to help you unscramble the following words:

1. oodlf ______
2. lhia _____
3. rrhunieac __________
4. sbrsu erfi ______ ____
5. der dtei ___ ____
6. qmsuotio _________
7. tsrfo ______
8. notorad ________
9. qethkaruea ____________
10. twspareuot ____________

WORD BANK

tornado
earthquake
brush fire
mosquito
hurricane
red tide
waterspout
hail
flood
frost

ANSWERS: 1.flood, 2.hail, 3.hurricane, 4.brush fire, 5.red tide, 6.mosquito, 7.frost, 8.tornado, 9.earthquake, 10.waterspout

Seashells of Sanibel Island

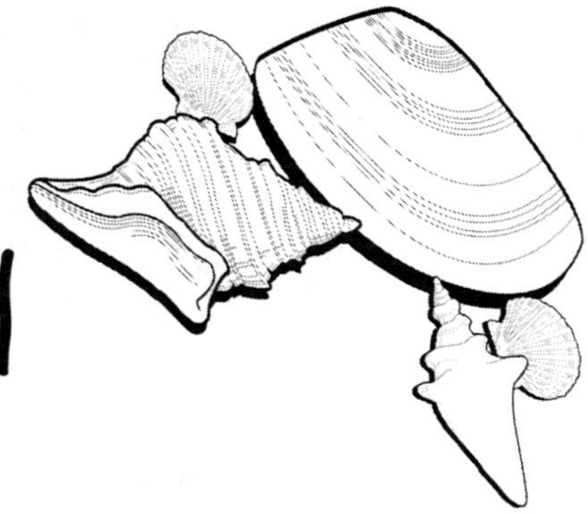

On the western coast of Florida, near Fort Myers, delightful Sanibel Island beckons weary visitors to its beautiful paradise. According to legend, rugged pirate, José Gasparilla, made Sanibel his home and named the island for a Spanish queen he ordained as Santa Isabella. Only 12 miles (19 kilometers) long, Sanibel Island is famous for its seashells that draw hundreds of visitors daily. Some of the shells sightseers might stumble upon are chilton, limpet, abalone, cerith, periwinkle, conch, cone, and auger.

A *haiku* is a three line poem with a certain number of syllables in each line. Look at the example below:

	1 2 3 4 5
The first line has 5 syllables	San/i/bel Is/land
	1 2 3 4 5 6 7
The second line has 7 syllables	Sun, sand, and sea/shells ga/lore
	1 2 3 4 5
The third line has 5 syllables	Come, see for your/self!

Now, write your own *haiku* about beautiful Sanibel Island!

____

____

____

Alligators Abound

American alligators were once nearly wiped out because of their hides and meat, but have since made a comeback all across Florida. The population of American alligators in Florida tops 1 million!

You can make at least 15 words from the letters in ALLIGATOR. See if you can find all 15–or more!

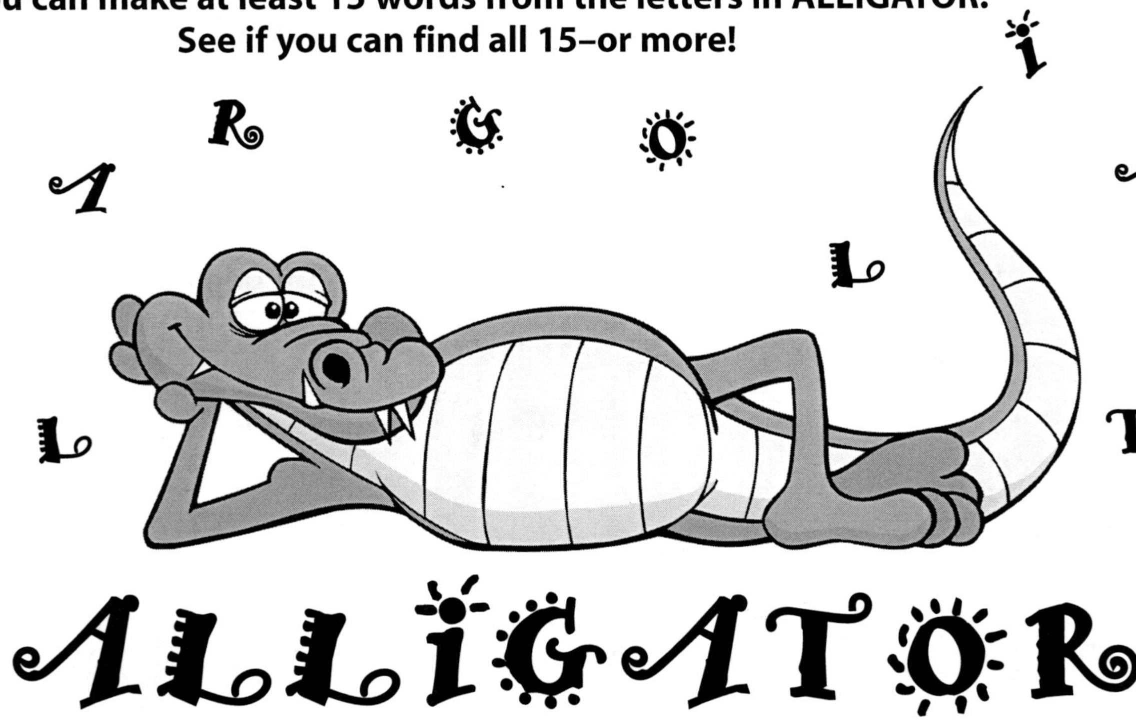

ANSWERS: 1. all 2. tall 3. rat 4. tag 5. rag 6. lag 7. at 8. it 9. or 10. go 11. to 12. log 13. gall 14. till 15. gill

Ponce de León And His Youthful Outlook

Spanish explorer, Juan Ponce de León, was the first European to set foot on the North American continent. Landing in the new country on March 27, 1513, Ponce de León named it Florida, which in Spanish means "full of flowers." Ponce de León had previously explored and conquered Puerto Rico in 1508. Sent by Spain to find gold and new settlements, Ponce de León was also searching for something himself.

What was Ponce de León looking for? Use this chart below to search out his mysterious quest.

A	B	C	D	E	F	G	H	I	J	K	L	M	N
8	26	18	3	5	20	7	2	1	19	6	10	4	17

O	P	Q	R	S	T	U	V	W	X	Y	Z
13	22	24	9	16	11	25	15	23	12	21	14

___ ___ ___   ___ ___ ___ ___ ___ ___ ___ ___

11 2 5   20 13 25 17 11 8 1 17

___ ___   ___ ___ ___ ___ ___

13 20   21 13 25 11 2

Answer: The Fountain of Youth

Florida Through The Times

Many great things have happened in Florida throughout its history, both past and present. Chronicle the following important Florida events by solving math problems to find out the years in which they happened.

1. Spaniard Ponce de León explores and names Florida.	2-1=	3+2=	9-8=	3/1=
2. The English take control of Florida by trading Havana, Cuba to Spain for the region.	6-5=	1x7=	5+1=	3x1=
3. Florida becomes part of the United States.	5-4=	2x4=	9-7=	1x1=
4. Florida becomes the twenty-seventh state on March 3.	7-6=	16/2=	8/2=	10-5=
5. The Overseas Highway to the Florida Keys opens.	9-8=	7+2=	3/1=	4x2=
6. Explorer I, the first U.S. space satellite, is launched from Cape Canaveral.	3-2=	4+5=	9-4=	4x2=
7. The first spacecraft to land men on the moon, *Apollo II*, blasts off from Cape Canaveral.	8-7=	3+6=	3+3=	18/2=
8. Walt Disney World opens near Orlando.	4-3=	10-1=	9-2=	1/1=
9. Mariel Boatlift brings 120,000 Cuban refugees to Florida.	1+0=	6+3=	24/3=	11x0=
10. Xavier L. Suarez becomes the first Cuban-born person to be elected mayor of Miami.	6-5=	8+1=	16/2=	4+1=

ANSWERS: 1.1513, 2.1763, 3.1821, 4.1845, 5.1938, 6.1958, 7.1969, 8.1971, 9.1980, 10.1985

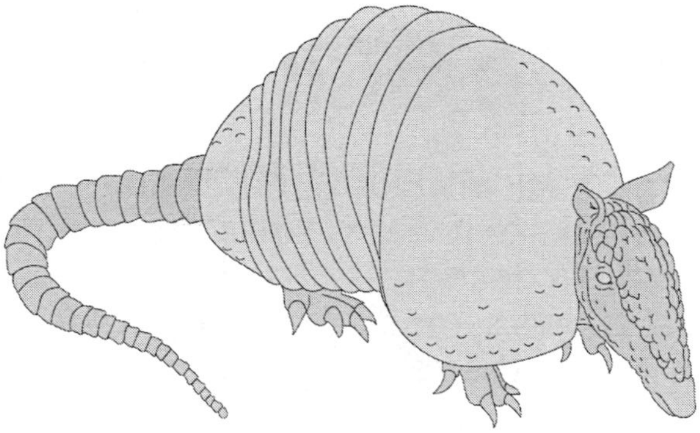

The Armored Armadillo

How are Florida's armadillos like a bullet proof vest? They have a defensive suit of armor already built in! Some armadillos can roll themselves into a ball so that they are completely covered in their armor. Their tongues are sticky like anteaters. That's how they pick up their food. Armadillos are usually nocturnal, which means they only come out at night. The legs and claws of the armadillo are especially suited for digging. Armadillos can bury themselves faster than you can chase them!

Fill in the blanks below using the word bank.

WORD BANK

night

suit of armor

legs

nocturnal

tongue

1. _ _ _ _ _ (_)
2. _ _ _ (_) _ _ _ _ _ _ _ _
3. _ _ _ (_) _
4. _ _ _ (_) _ _ _ _ _ _
5. _ (_) _ _

Now unscramble the "bubble" letters to discover the mystery word in the sentence below:

Armadillos have few or no _ _ _ _ _!

ANSWERS: 1. tongue, 2. suit of armor, 3. night, 4. nocturnal, 5. legs; Mystery word: teeth

Florida State Seal

The Legislature set up a basic design for our state seal back in 1868. But the early version had some mistakes like a steamboat that looked like it was sinking, mountains in the distance, and a Native American woman wearing a headdress of a male Native American from a different state. Today our state seal shows symbols of history, wildlife and industry. Just for fun, see if you can find which part of the seal symbolizes:

(1.) history, (2.) wildlife, and (3.) industry.

Color the state seal.

Answers: 1. Seminole woman 2. Sabal Palm 3. steamboat

Hardwood Hammocks

Tropical hardwood hammocks are found on the coastal ridges, islands, and on ground that is slightly raised above the marshes and wetlands.
Below is a list of words associated with the hardwood hammocks of Florida.

See if you can find the words in the word search

CANOPY
OVERSTORY
KEY LARGO
WEST INDIAN
TROPICAL
MIDSTORY
MARSHES
TREE SNAIL
KEYS
GUMBO-LIMBO

W E S T I N D I A N M
M O K T C V R K C T A
I T E V C B Q E A R R
D T Y C K E N Y N O S
S E S U O Y G L O P H
T O R P I L C A P I E
O V E R S T O R Y C S
R G U L I B O G C A B
Y E T G L U T O O L K
T R E E S N A I L S V
G U M B O L I M B O P

Sea Habitat

Why do sea animals live where they do?

Sea animals need good surroundings just like we do! Florida provides ample seas and a wonderful climate for its sea animals. At times, to the sea animals, the sea can seem like a vast bowl of soup. Sometimes you can see dolphins in a feeding frenzy. They surface for air and dive for food. Eating is not the only thing that determines where sea animals live. Temperature, salinity, and breeding habitat all affect where sea animals live.

Put the following Florida sea animals in alphabetical order.

_____ skate

_____ tarpon

_____ eel

_____ squid

_____ turtle

_____ dolphin

_____ shark

_____ ray

_____ tuna

_____ blue marlin

ANSWERS: 1.blue marlin 2.dolphin 3.eel 4.ray 5.shark 6.skate 7.squid 8.tarpon 9.tuna 10.turtle

Florida Word Wheel

From the Word Wheel of Florida names, answer the following questions.

1. The largest river in Florida is the ______________________________. Can you believe it flows from south to north?!
2. Land that is surrounded by water on three sides is called a ____________________.
3. The Florida football team that won the Super Bowl in 1973 and 1974 is the ____________________________________.
4. The town named after a Calusa Indian word that contains the two words "kiss me" is __________________________________.
5. __________________________ led the Seminoles in their fight to remain in Florida.
6. Many treasure hunters travel to the _________________________ to look for sunken vessels.
7. The country's "winter baseball capital" is _________________________.
8. One of the largest pizzas of all time was made in 1991 in ____________________. It had 120,000 slices and was eaten by 30,000 people!
9. Not far from Orlando is a town named after a well known holiday. The town is named _____________________________.
10. Did you know that school kids picked the state animal, the ___________________.

ANSWERS: 1. St. Johns River 2. peninsula 3. Miami Dolphins 4. Kissimmee 5. Osceola 6. Florida Keys 7. St. Petersburg 8. Tallahassee 9. Christmas 10. panther

Ahoy, Mate, Is That Land I See?

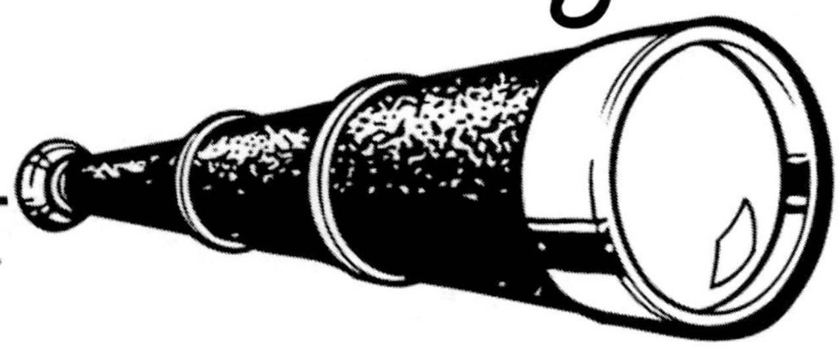

Pretend you are a Spanish explorer sent to discover the New World. Your ship is off the coast of Florida. After many months aboard a ship, you finally spy land. You are writing the day's entry in the ship's log book. Describe what you see as you gaze at the Florida coast.

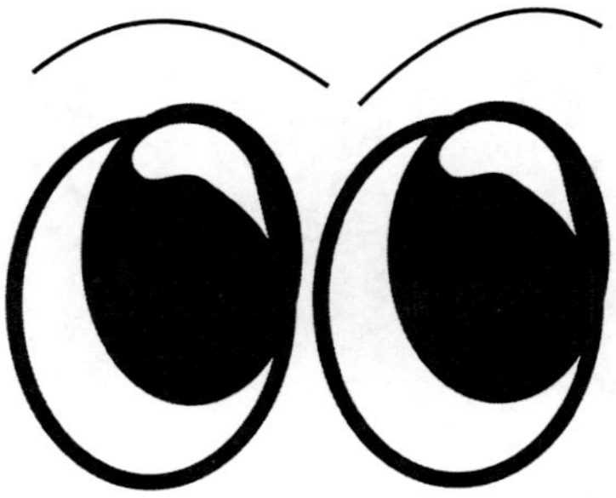

Looking For a Home!

Match the things on the left with a home on the right!

1. "mermaid"
2. floundering fish
3. lighthouse keeper
4. ship at sea
5. American alligator
6. Florida ghost
7. space shuttle
8. lost commuter

A. Atlantic Ocean

B. Cape Canaveral

C. Eastern Shore net

D. A haunted Florida house

E. Alligator Reef Lighthouse

F. Marshes and springs

G. Glass-bottomed boat at Weeki Wachee

H. Interstate 95

ANSWERS: 1.G, 2.C, 3.E, 4.A, 5.F, 6.D, 7.B, 8.H

Make A Seminole Indian Vest!

Indians in Florida wore clothing that was made from the skins of deer.

To make your deerskin vest, you will need a brown paper bag. Lay the bag flat as shown in the picture. Cut out holes for your arms and neck. Make a long slit in one side of the bag.

Ideas for decorating your vest:

- glue buttons, glitter, and feathers on the vest
- use markers or crayons to draw Indian symbols on the vest
- make fringe at the bottom of the bag by snipping along the edges of the bag
- decorate your vest with beads, shells, etc.

Get together with your friends and have a great "pow-wow!"

Florida Fun Foods

Take a break, Mom! We can make snacks on our own. Try each of the following recipes.

SANDY BEACH TOAST

Ingredients:
Slice or two of fresh bread
Butter or margarine
Cinnamon
Sugar

Directions:
Toast bread, lightly butter, then sprinkle cinnamon and sugar on top.
You can even mix the cinnamon and sugar first if you want. ENJOY!

ALLIGATORS

Ingredients:
4 inch pieces of clean celery
Cream cheese or peanut butter
Chopped nuts
Few raisins

Directions:
Fill pieces of celery with either peanut butter or cream cheese.
Decorate with chopped nuts and use 2 raisins for the eyes.

ENJOY!

The Delightful Dolphin

Dolphins are mammals that often swim close to Florida's shoreline. They are very friendly animals that travel in large groups. Known for their intelligence, dolphins communicate with each other by whistling and squealing. If one of their group members is injured, the dolphin will help it to the surface so that it can breathe.

Color the dolphin jumping high above the ocean waves. You can even color a boat or the beach in the background!

A Florida Harvest

Match the name of each crop or product from Florida with the picture of that item.

cotton peanuts berries eggs

crabs and fish grapes

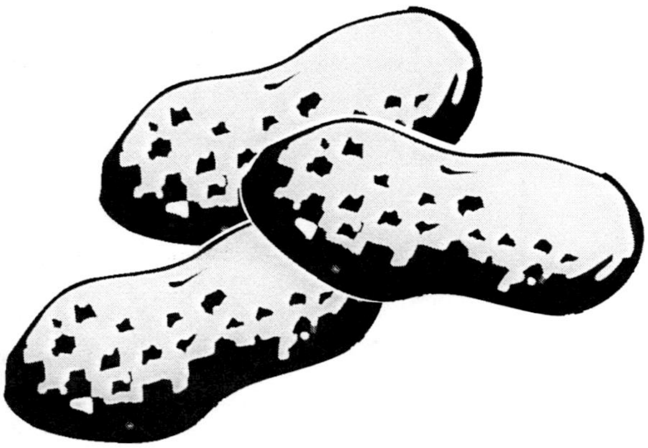

3...2...1...Blast Off!

In 1950 the U.S. Air Force began testing missiles at Cape Canaveral. Less than ten years later, the National Aeronautics and Space Administration (NASA) launched *Explorer I*, the first U.S. satellite to orbit the earth.
Many historic launches have blasted off from Cape Canaveral since 1958. Among them were *Apollo II* in 1969, when Neil Armstrong became the first person to walk on the moon, and the *Challenger* in 1983, when Sally Ride became the first American woman in space.

Color the astronaut.

Florida State Greats!

How many of these State Greats from the Great State of Florida do you know?

Use an encyclopedia, almanac, or other resource to match the following facts with the State Great they describe.

Hint: There are two facts for each State Great!

____ 1. industrialist who built the overseas railway

____ 2. first known professional European artist to visit the continental United States

____ 3. First African-American woman elected to the Florida State Legislature

____ 4. owned a coconut plantation

____ 5. gave Europeans some of their earliest exposure to Native-American life

____ 6. politician who was instrumental in the drainage of the Everglades

____ 7. famous physician and inventor

____ 8. instituted consolidated university system

____ 9. first African-American to attend the University of Miami Law School

____ 10. began the development of Miami Beach as a tourist center

____ 11. responsible for railroad and hotel development of Florida's east coast

____ 12. patented a refrigeration system for the sickrooms of fever patients

STATE GREAT

A. Jacques de Morgues Le Moyne

B. Napoleon Broward

C. Gwendolyn Sawyer Cherry

D. John. S. Collins

E. John Gorrie

F. Henry Flagler

ANSWERS: 1.F, 2.A, 3.C, 4.D, 5.A, 6.B, 7.E, 8.B, 9.C, 10.D, 11.F, 12.E

The Scenic Route

Imagine that you are leading a group on a tour of famous Florida landmarks. Circle the following places on the map below, then number them in the order you would visit them if you were traveling from north to south.

HINT: The first two have been done for you!

_____ University of Florida (Gainesville)

_____ John F. Kennedy Space Center (Cape Canaveral)

_____ Disney World (near Orlando)

_____ John Penne Kamp Coral Reef (near Key Largo)

_____ Busch Gardens (Tampa)

_____ Overseas Highway (between Key Largo Key West)

_____ Daytona International Speedway (Daytona)

__1__ State capitol building (Tallahassee)

_____ Everglades National Park (between Naples and Miami)

__2__ Castillo de San Marcos (St. Augustine)

ANSWERS: 3, 6, 5, 9, 7, 10, 4, 1, 8, 2

David Levy Yulee

David Levy Yulee was one of Florida's first two U.S. Senators. First elected to the senate in 1845, Yulee served until 1851 and served again from 1855 to 1861. Yulee labored hard to gain statehood for Florida and was pleased when Florida became a state on March 3, 1845.

Fill in the missing words.

**Cross out every other letter below, beginning with the second one.
The letters that remain will answer the question.**

J J E T W Z I Q S X H

1. Yulee was the first __ __ __ __ __ __ member of the Senate.

R X A P I M L F R W O D A C D

2. In the 1860s, Yulee founded Florida's first __ __ __ __ __ __ __ __ that crossed the Atlantic to the Gulf.

L Q E T V S Y   Y O U B L M E S E

3. Both __ __ __ __ County and the town of __ __ __ __ __ are named in his honor.

ANSWERS: 1. JEWISH, 2. RAILROAD, 3. LEVY, YULEE

Shoot For The Stars

Ray Charles

Ray Charles is a wonderful example of an African-American overcoming obstacles to reach the top. He is one of Florida's most successful and well-known entertainers.

Born into poverty, Charles moved many times as a child. His family was so poor that they had no indoor plumbing. Because his father was not around very much, his mother had to be the strong disciplinarian. She taught him not to beg, cheat, or steal. He learned early to work hard for what he wanted.

Ray Charles loved to bang around on the piano keys when he was a child. At 5 he started to lose his eyesight and within 2 years, was blind. His mother sent him away to school in St. Augustine to learn Braille, and it was there that he had his first formal piano lessons.

Because Ray Charles worked so hard to overcome his problems in early life, he has become one of the most famous entertainers in America. Disabilities don't have to keep dreams from coming true!

Write down the meaning of each of the following words:

1. entertainer ______________________________________
2. disciplinarian ______________________________________
3. obstacles ______________________________________
4. Braille ______________________________________
5. famous ______________________________________
6. disabilities ______________________________________

Florida's Fabulous Fronds

Our state tree reminds us that our roots should run deep if we want to grow straight and tall! The state tree for Florida is the Sabal Palm. It grows throughout the state. In early days it provided both food and shelter for the settlers. The young buds were eaten, the trunks were cut into logs for the walls of forts and homes, and the leaves were made into roof thatching.

Color the Sabal Palm.

Zebra Longwings

Our state butterfly is the zebra longwing. You may have guessed that the zebra longwing got its name because it is striped like a zebra and has very long wings. Did you know that they live with their relatives in flocks, or that each butterfly has its own favorite "perch" where it returns to sleep each night? If you want to see the zebra longwing, visit the Everglades National Park.

Using the Word Bank to the right, fill in the blanks below:

WORD BANK

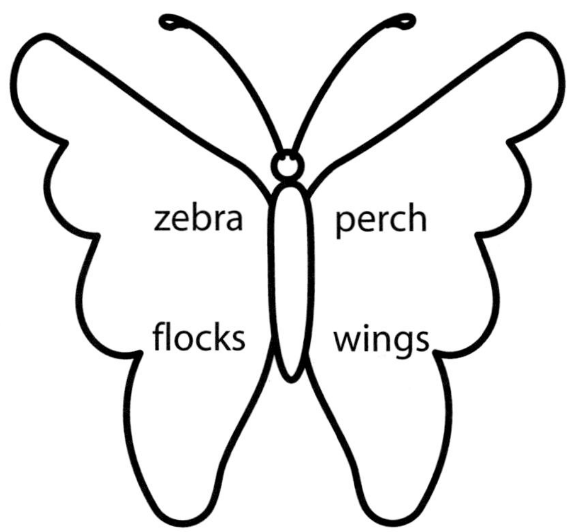

1. ___ ___ b ___ (___)

2. ___ l ___ ___ (___) ___

3. ___ (___) r ___ ___

4. (___) ___ ___ g ___

Now unscramble the bubble letters to find the mystery word below:

The zebra longwing is actually a ___ ___ ___ ___ flyer.

ANSWER: 1. zebra, 2. flocks, 3. perch, 4. wings,
Mystery word: weak

Famous Florida Folks Scavenger Hunt

Here is a list of just some of the famous people from our state. Go on a scavenger hunt to see if you can "capture" a fact about each one. Use an encyclopedia, almanac, or other resource you might need. Happy hunting!

FAMOUS PERSON	FAMOUS FACT
Juan Ponce de León	________________
Hernando de Soto	________________
Timucuans	________________
William Duval	________________
Osceola	________________
David Yulee	________________
Henry Flagler	________________
Carl Fisher	________________
Walt Disney	________________
Vincente Ybor	________________
John Ringling	________________
Janet Reno	________________
Thomas Edison	________________
Henry Ford	________________
John Gorrie	________________
Miccosukee	________________
Mary McLeod Bethune	________________
Chris Evert Loyd	________________
Marjorie Kinnan Rawlings	________________
Ernest Hemingway	________________
Sidney Poitier	________________
John James Audubon	________________
Highwaymen	________________
Claude Pepper	________________

Florida People

A state is not just towns and mountains and rivers. A state is its people! But the really important people in a state are not famous. You may know them—they may be your mom, your dad, or your teacher. The average, everyday person is the one who makes the state a good state. How? By working hard, by paying taxes, by voting, and by helping Florida children grow up to be good state citizens!

Match each Florida person with their accomplishment.

1. Osceola	A. publisher
2. Chris Evert-Lloyd	B. labor leader
3. Frank Doubleday	C. 1st female Attorney General
4. John James Audubon	D. circus owners
5. A. Phillip Randolph	E. musician
6. Janet Reno	F. educator
7. John & Charles Ringling	G. inventor of refrigeration
8. John Gorrie	H. author
9. Marjorie Kinnan Rawlings	I. author
10. Zora Neale Hurston	J. Seminole leader
11. Julian "Cannonball" Adderley	K. artist, Ornithologist
12. Mary McLeod Bethune	L. tennis champion

Answers: 1–J; 2–L; 3–A; 4–K; 5–B; 6–C; 7–D; 8–G; 9–H; 10–I; 11–E; 12–F

Florida Gazetteer

A gazetteer is a list of places. Use the word bank to complete the names of some of these famous places in our state:

1. _ _ _ West
2. _ _ _ _ _ Beach
3. _ _ _ _ Cypress
4. _ _ _ _ _ _ Gables
5. _ _ _ _ _ Dora
6. _ _ _ _ _ _ _ _ Bay
7. Tarpon _ _ _ _ _ _ _
8. _ _ _ _ Beach
9. _ _ _ _ _ _ _ Island
10. Castillo _ _ _ _ _ Marcos

WORD BANK

Mount	de San
Miami	Big
Palm	Biscayne
Springs	Coral
Key	Merritt

ANSWERS: 1.Key, 2.Miami, 3.Big, 4.Coral, 5.Mount, 6.Biscayne, 7.Springs, 8.Palm, 9.Merritt, 10.de San

Florida Trivia

There are about 30,000 lakes in Florida.

The world's smallest police station is a telephone booth in Carabelle.

Author Ernest Hemingway's home and museum is in Key West.

Nearly half of Florida is covered with uninhabited forest.

The brilliant white sand on northwest Florida beaches is 99% pure quartz crystal formed in the Appalachian mountains, then ground, polished, and bleached during its long journey downriver to the Gulf of Mexico.

Sanibel Island is known as one of the best shelling beaches on earth.

The port of Miami is the busiest cruise port in the U.S.

Florida is the only state which has two rivers with the same name. There is Withlacoochee in north central Florida and one in central Florida. They are not connected in any way. They just have the same name.

Key West has the highest average temperature in the U.S.

Today there are four federal Indian reservations in Florida. The major tribes include: Seminole, Miccosukee, and Cherokee.

The lowest point in Florida is the Atlantic Ocean at sea level.

Orlando has more visitors than any other amusement park destination in the U.S.

Add another fact that you know here:______________________________

Illuminating Florida!

Famous inventor Thomas Alva Edison was so impressed with the natural beauty of Fort Myers that he and his new bride made Fort Myers their winter home. Edison built a laboratory in Fort Myers where he used many plants from around the world in his inventions. Bamboo was used as a filament for his lamps. A filament is the slender wiring inside a bulb that causes a bulb to blow out! Edison issued more than 1,000 patents during his career.

Fill in the missing letters to see how many inventions you can name. Some of the consonants have been supplied for you.

1. P h _ n _ g _ _ _ _ _
2. _ n c _ _ d _ _ _ _ n t   _ _ m p
3. m _ v _ n g   p _ _ t _ r _   c _ m _ r _
4. s t _ _ k   t _ c k _ r
5. d _ p _ _ x and quadruplex t _ l _ g r _ _ _ s
6. k _ n _ t o _ c _ p _

Answers: 1. phonograph, 2. incandescent lamp, 3. moving picture camera, 4. stock ticker, 5. diplex, telegraphs, 6. kinetoscope

Getting Back To Nature

Natural resources are things that exist or are formed by nature.

Some of Florida's natural resources are its trees, phosphate deposits, petroleum, fuller's earth, coquina rock, fish and shellfish, and fruit. Manufacturers in Florida use many of these natural resources to make finished products. For example, coquina rock was one of the most popular construction materials during Florida's boom days. It is a type of limestone composed of broken coral and sea shells.

How many products can you think of that can be made from Florida's natural resources?

Where Are Flamingo's Flamingos?

Over the years many people have wondered if flamingos like to visit the town of Flamingo, Florida. Until the early 1900s, several hundred flamingos would migrate from their summer breeding grounds in the Bahamas to the Florida Bay for the winter. Today most sightings of the flamingos in Flamingo are attributed to birds who escaped Miami area attractions. Flocks of up to 30 birds have been sighted in Florida Bay and Snake Bite.The reason for the dwindling number of birds coming to Flamingo each winter is probably because of the loss of nesting sites in the area due to development.

See how many flamingos you can sight in Flamingo

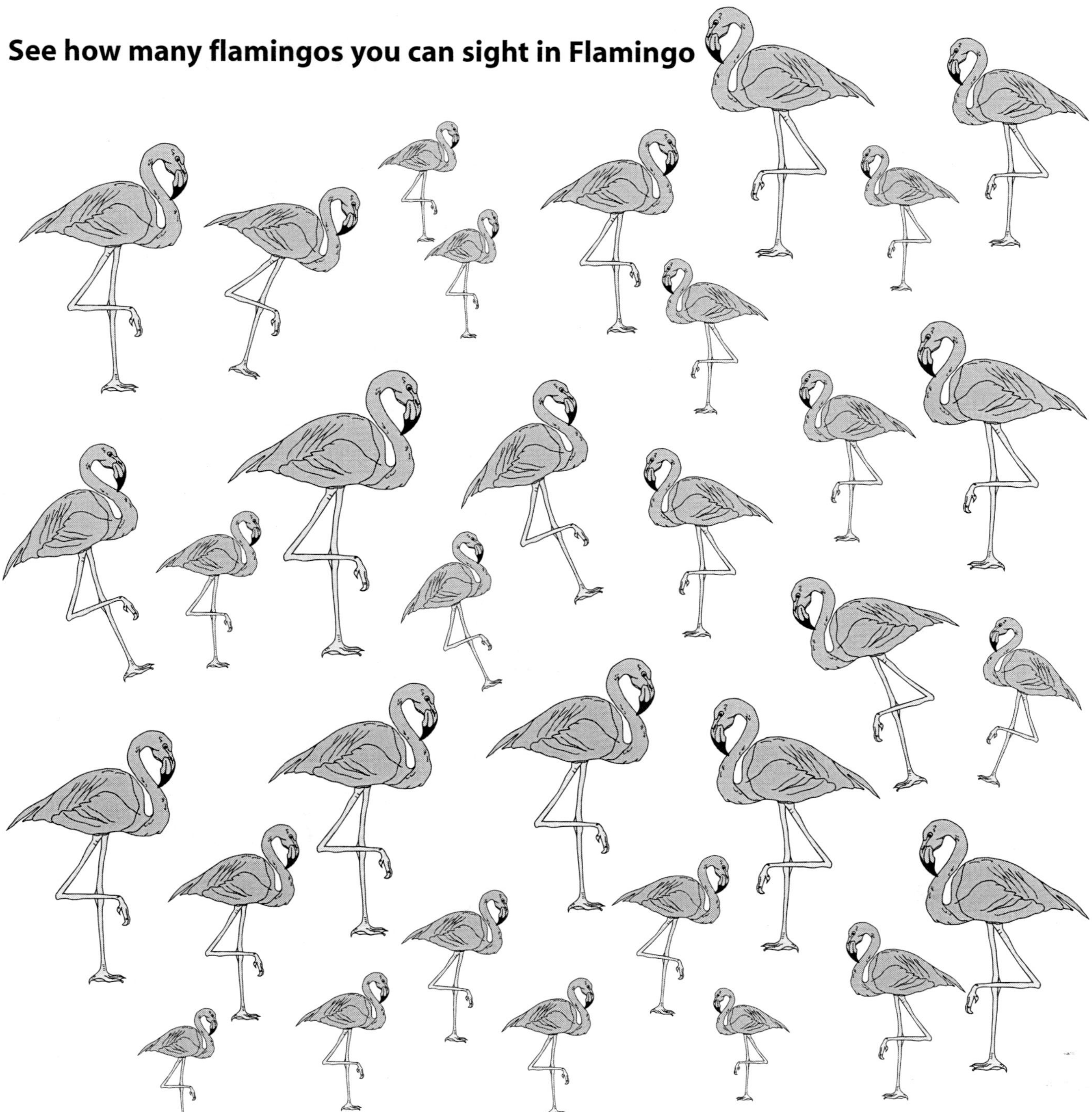

Answer: 32

Unique Florida Place Names

Match the name of these towns with their descriptions.

____ Cape Canaveral

____ Neptune Beach

____ Treasure Island

____ Tarpon Springs

____ St. Augustine

____ Palm Beach

____ Jacksonville

____ Mount Dora

____ Tallahassee

____ Pensacola

A. home to the Riverwalk on the St. Johns River

B. Florida's capital

C. on a barrier island changed by Flagler

D. home of space launches

E. home of a naval air station

F. oldest city in U.S.

G. sponge fishing center

H. town named after a planet

I. town known for its sand castles

J. low lakeside bluff

Answer: D, H, I, G, F, C, A, J, B, E

Florida State Song

Florida's state song, "Old Folks at Home," was written by Stephen Collins Foster and adopted as the official state song in 1935. Although he had never seen the Suwannee River, or "Swanee" as he called it, Foster's beautiful lyrics add to the mystic beauty of the river.

"Old Folks at Home"
Stephen Collins Foster

Way down upon the Swanee River
Far, far away
There's where my heart is turning ever,
There's where the old folks stay.
All up and down the whole creation
Sadly I roam,
Still longing for the old plantation,
And for the old folks at home.

(CHORUS)
All the world is sad and dreary,
Everywhere I roam;
Oh brothers, how my heart grows weary,
Far from the old folks at home!

While reading the words of the song, you'll notice that Foster used words that rhymed.

Try writing your own verse that rhymes. Use the list of rhyming words below or think of rhyming words on your own. Then, add your verse to the bottom of the state song. Remember, have a good time as you rhyme!

RHYMING WORDS

river	shore	sang
quiver	adore	twang
sliver	lore	bang
liver	snore	hang

Read instructions to the right of the page.
Write your new verse below:

____

____

____

____

____

____

____

Florida Timeline: A Short & Sweet History Of Our State

The varied time periods of Florida's timeline have added to the richness of our history.

Look at the mixed-up timeline below and put the time periods in their correct chronological order. Number them from 1 to 9 with 1 being the first time period occurring in Florida history. The first two have been done for you.

_____ First Seminole War

_____ Florida becomes a state

__1__ Juan Ponce de León arrives

_____ Hurricane Andrew

__2__ St. Augustine settled

_____ Florida becomes U.S. territory

_____ Missile test center established in Cape Canaveral

_____ Florida's sixth constitution established

_____ Florida secedes from the Union

Answers: 3, 5, 1, 10, 2, 4, 7, 8, 6

Save the Birds!

Florida is home to a wide variety of birds; so many that John James Audubon found the state to be an excellent place to study and paint all the different kinds. Up until the early 1900s, millions of wading birds could be observed nesting and feeding in Florida's wetlands. In 1905, legal protection had to be enforced to save the birds which were being hunted to near extinction for their beautiful feathers.
Some of the birds you might see in Florida today include the brown pelican, great white heron, osprey, peregrine falcon, pileated woodpecker, piping plover, purple gallinule, roseate spoonbill, snail kite, southern bald eagle, tricolored heron, white-crowned pigeon, white pelican, and wood stork.

You can enjoy feeding the birds in your own neighborhood by making a bird feeder. Then, sit back and enjoy the beauty of birds as they fly in for a snack.

Materials:

1 empty, clean 1/2 gallon orange juice carton
1 pair of pointed, sharp scissors
1 wooden stick or tree limb, 10 to 12 inches long
1 large paper clip
1 bag of birdseed
1 six inch piece of yarn or string

Instructions:

1. With sharp scissors, cut doors in the center of carton, leaving 1/2" to 1" border.
2. Cut a small 1/2" hole underneath both door frames, then slide stick through the holes to create a perch.
3. Open paper clip to make hook, then make a small hole at the top of carton and push hook through opening.
4. Add birdseed to feeder.
5. String yarn through top of hook and tie feeder to tree branch, making sure it is safe from predators.

Life On The Reef

The only living coral reef system in North America is off the Atlantic coast side of the Florida Keys. Coral reefs are made up of thousands of microscopic animals called polyps. These polyps collect calcium from the sea water around them and turn it into a "skeleton." Over the years, more polyps come along and make more "skeletons" on top of, or beside, the older ones. Coral reefs are made from the many skeletons of polyps.

Because the coral reef has so many ledges, holes, and crevices, it is a perfect place for shrimp, crabs, turtles, lobsters, and many kinds of fish to live.

Circle the critters that would not live on a reef.